Fi Kirkpatrick has lived in London since 1991 and has cooked for virtually everybody within the M25 corridor. She has worked in publishing and management consultancy, but her love of cooking and entertaining, inspired in her from the cradle, remain her priority. She has a degree in French from Edinburgh University, which has come in very handy for restaurant menus!

****

Dominic Finn has been entertaining "as easily as possible" for 10 years. Since leaving the world of finance, he has written for magazines and is now writing a sitcom. After living in the North East of England, Dublin and Scotland he is now a resident of Islington.

Debrett's

NEW GUIDE TO EASY ENTERTAINING

Fi Kirkpatrick and Dominic Finn

DEBRETT'S PEERAGE LTD

Copyright 2000 Debrett's Peerage Limited
Debrett Trade Mark Copyright © 2000 Debrett's Peerage Limited

The right of Fi Kirkpatrick and Dominic Finn to be identified as the Authors of this work has been asserted by them in accordance with the Copyright, Designs and Patent Act 1988

First published in 2000 by Debrett's Peerage Limited

All rights reserved. No part of this book may be reproduced, stored in a retrieval system, or transmitted, in any form or by any means without the prior written permission of the publisher, nor be otherwise circulated in any form of binding or cover other than that in which it is published and without a similar condition being imposed on the subsequent purchaser.

Debrett's Peerage Limited wishes to make clear that the views expressed in this book are the Authors' own, and any correspondence should be addressed directly to them via the publishers.

British Library Cataloguing in Publication Data

ISBN 1 870520 84 X

Printed and bound in Great Britain by
Polestar Wheatons Ltd, Exeter

Debrett's Peerage Limited
Kings Court, 2–16 Goodge Street, London W1T 2QA
www.debretts.co.uk e-mail people@debretts.co.uk

Debrett's Peerage Limited was founded in 1769 when George III was on the throne, and is one of the oldest and most established names in publishing in the UK. Debrett's has traditionally been best known for its **Peerage and Baronetage** produced under licence by Macmillan; the next edition will be published in the year 2003. **Debrett's People of Today**, however, the annual biographical reference source for contemporary Britain first published in 1988, has rapidly become a flagship product for the company. Debrett's is now a modern publisher with a long list of titles including:

- Debrett's Correct Form
- Debrett's New Guide to Etiquette and Modern Manners
- Debrett's Wedding Guide
- Debrett's Guide to Tracing your Family Tree

The Debrett's name is seen as a unique and authoritative guide to all aspects of social custom in the UK.

Thank you to John Wheatley, without whom this book would never have been written; to the IT department in my office for letting me blag a laptop so I could work on this book instead of doing my job; to Boris Starling, owner of the most ruthlessly efficient printer in Bayswater; and to Lucy Henry, for general all-round heroic endurance. You know where the bodies are buried. And finally to my mother, whose great food in the face of much anti-vegetable sentiment from my brother inspired me to set off on my own. Thanks Mum, and I still think 'velvet steak' is the best name for liver I've ever heard.

FK

Contents

Introduction	xi
Before You Begin	**1**
Equipment	1
Kitchen Gadgets	3
Store Cupboard Basics	3
Freezer	6
Breakfast	**7**
The Working Breakfast	8
Brunch	9
Lunch	**18**
Lunch Invitations	20
Traditional Sunday Lunch	25
Business and Working Lunches	30
Weekend Lunches	30
Inviting Children to Lunch	34
Tea	**43**
The Meal	43
The Drink	49
Invitations	49
Supper	**50**
When	52
Food	52
Late Leaving Guests	52
Cleaning Up	52
Dinner Parties	**55**
The Theory	59
The Basics	59
Guest Lists	60
Preparation	60
How to Invite	61
The Implication of Your Invitation	62

Contents

Technology	62
Other Considerations	63
Replies	63
Catering for Fussy Eaters	71
Pear Shaped Meals	80
Proportion of Pre-cooked Food	80
Table Talk	81

Drinks — 82
Pre-Dinner Drinks	82
Drinks During Dinner	83
Quality and Quantity	83
Temperatures	84
What Goes with What	84
Bringing Wine	85
Port & Spirits	85
Coffee	86
Smoking	86
Drunks	87

Parties — 89
Canapés	89
Buffets	94

House Parties — 102

Cooking in the Open Air — 108
Barbecues	108
Alfresco	112
Picnics	112
Walking Picnic	114
Car Boot Picnic	116

Impromptu Entertaining — 121
What to Throw Together from the Cupboard	124

Cooking to Impress — 136
Impressing a Boss	140
Impressing a Potential Partner	141

Conclusion — 143

List of Recipes — 144

Introduction

If you are just looking for a cookbook, then this is not the book for you. Book shops and library shelves are laden with an abundance of gastronomic inventiveness, but our experience tells us that warm, friendly, and successful entertaining arises from more than just the right Muscadet with the fish course. It is far more about hard work and planning; this sounds mundane but if this is executed skilfully you will receive great personal reward and satisfaction.

It is true to say that many actions are influenced by 'form'. There are many books on the social 'do's and don'ts', but this book is more concerned with the ease of modern entertaining than its social correctness. Entertaining is both an art and a science, and involves careful thought and planning.

Many of us nowadays have full-time jobs, a social life and a very impatient attitude. We seldom have the time or the desire to spend three hours making lamb stock from scratch as one component of one dish which is only part of a hugely elaborate eight-course meal. Things like that are best left to restaurants where they have the time and the resources (and the massive quantities of lamb bones) to do this as a matter of routine. Many of us have concluded that we must play to our strengths. If you know you are not very good in the kitchen, buy food in. The bottom line is, the people you have invited to your house are there to see you, and not to judge you on the crispness of your pastry. Just cook them something delicious, because you want them at your table; they are not Egon Ronay inspectors. It's supposed to be fun, not an ordeal. If you are relaxed about what you're giving them, then they will be too, and everyone will have a good time. This book is designed to help you to relax in the kitchen and to assist you in turning a crisis into an opportunity.

"Better is a dinner of herbs where love is, than a stalled ox and hatred therewith"

So why do we entertain? If your motive for entertaining is more than just having a few close friends and family over to

Introduction

sample a new dish, then do not judge yourself harshly. Mixing food within a social context has been the catalyst for social advancement for thousands of years. Kings have used the process of 'breaking bread' to push the boundaries of their fiefdoms. A successful Venetian merchant wishing to marry an aristocrat's daughter would invite her family to sip wine on his terrace overlooking the Rialto. A struggling artist may use a dinner to reassure his wife's family that she will not starve.

In a modern context, a city banker may wish to show her boss her new Sotheby's acquisition. As he sits on her Bugatti chair, which she has paid for out of last year's bonus, she will use the opportunity to lobby for better pay and perks. Your motivation will be entirely personal, business or pleasure, or in the majority of cases, both.

Before You Begin

Equipment

One thing I will say, and it is a cliché I'm afraid, is that it is important to have good equipment. You don't need masses of gadgets – it's better to be selective. I own a Mouli vegetable mill, a fish kettle and a potato ricer, and have relegated them to the top of the kitchen cupboard where they have remained untouched for two and a half years, but on the other hand my food processor, microwave and stacking steamer baskets are involved in almost every meal. Trial and error – and time spent in the kitchen – will tell you what you need.

Good, sharp knives are important, and I really only use two with any regularity – a three-inch Sabatier vegetable knife; and a six-inch Kitchen Devils general all-purpose one which gets used for chopping onions, carving roast joints, scoring pastry – everything in fact that the little knife (known in my kitchen as 'Naughty Knife', because it is very small and wickedly sharp) doesn't do. I also have a pair of really sturdy kitchen scissors which I use for everything. The two main uses they have though, which are strictly non cordon bleu approved, are for chopping herbs (stuff the sprigs of parsley into a mug and hack them up with the scissors); and for cutting up raw chicken breasts and rashers of bacon – so much easier than a knife. I have a non-stick frying pan, and a non-stick saucepan with two handles and a lid which can go straight from the hob into the oven, which is ideal for making stews and casseroles. Now is the time to say that I do not own any of that well-known make of cast-iron enamelled cookware – yes, you know the one I mean – it's brutally expensive so everyone has it on their wedding list. It's all delightfully rustic and yes, I daresay it does a grand job of making casseroles – but have you ever tried to lift one when it's holding enough boeuf bourguignon for eight people? Heavy is not the word. Life is difficult enough without giving yourself a hernia just making supper. Don't do it.

Having completely castigated cast iron, I do own one of those ridged griddles – brilliant for making a couple of hastily marinated chicken breasts and some peppers look like you've really tried – and a couple of heavy saucepans for boiling pasta or vegetables. Oh and while I'm here, if there are any saucepan manufacturers reading – it is the world's most annoying thing (right up there with the gratuitous apostrophe use by green-grocers, as in 'cabbage's 20p a pound') to have a pouring lip on a saucepan ON THE WRONG SIDE. Which they ALL are – unless you're left handed, which only 10% of the population is. I can understand why it's happened – the theory is that you lift the pan with your right hand and pour by tilting your wrist inwards – and yes, if that is indeed what you are doing, then the lip is correctly positioned on the left-hand rim of the pan. However, 99% of the time you have made something which needs to be helped out of the pot – with a spatula, or a wooden spoon – so what do you do? Lift the pan with your left hand, tilt your wrist and scrape with your right hand. And the pouring lip is left laughing at you from the wrong side of the pan. For goodness sake! The whole thing has clearly been designed by a man who never goes into the kitchen.

Anyway, I seem to have strayed off the point rather. Back to the equipment. For oven use, I recommend a good heavy roasting tin with high sides; a square non-stick baking sheet with a tiny (3mm) lip; and a pretty blue and white china rectangular lasagne dish which does all sorts of things – baked custards, pommes dauphinoises, roasted green beans, lemon surprise pudding. Also highly recommended is a 12-inch metal tart tin with fluted edges and a removable base (which rather handily sits nicely on the non-stick baking sheet. This is useful for two reasons: first, if you pre-heat the baking sheet and then put the filled tart tin on the hot sheet in the oven, it gives it a really good blast of heat which helps to make the pastry base really crisp; secondly, and no less importantly, have you ever tried gripping a red hot tart with a pair of oven gloves when the only bit you can grip for fear of breaking your beautiful brown and crispy fluted pastry edges is the thin sliver of metal showing round the bottom? I rest my case.

The final bit of equipment I use most often may seem a

little gratuitous, but it has got to be the easiest instant pudding maker I know: my ice cream machine. I don't have the fancy free-standing type (more's the pity), but the basic £40-worth of tub plus clip-on churning motor. I keep the tub in the freezer so it's always ready to go, and assuming your ingredients are cold to start with you can have ice cream or sorbet in half an hour. And you can use anything. Yoghurt, fruit juice, cream, milk, custard, mascarpone, pureed fruit, chocolate chips – anything. It's brilliant.

Most people accumulate kitchen equipment over a number of years, so nothing really matches, but if you are a keen cook this will not matter to you. Yes, the battered old roasting tin doesn't go with the casserole dish, but it is the perfect size for your lamb boulangère, plus you know it doesn't stick on the bottom as the new one does. The items mentioned above are what I use most regularly and could not be without. Trial and error in your own kitchen is the only way you'll discover what works for you.

Kitchen Gadgets

Juicers, sandwich makers, waffle makers, fondue sets, raclette machines, woks, tall asparagus steamers, fish shaped pans, food processors, pasta machines with ravioli attachments.

Your kitchen may resemble a designer's dream, but many gadgets may go unused due to lack of wall outlets or sadly because the fashion is towards simplicity. Just because it is a gadget does not mean it's desirable or saves you time. Food warming trolleys are reminiscent of Margot in *The Good Life*. Whether you should use them depends on how well it keeps the food warm and seals in taste. If you have lots of dishes to do where the timing is difficult then perhaps they may serve a purpose; but perhaps you should simplify the menu, serve something cold or go out for dinner.

Store Cupboard Basics

The A List

If the worst comes to the worst, you will always be able to rustle up some form of food as long as you have (a) a bag of dried pasta; and (b) a jar of pasta sauce. Pesto; mushroom and bacon; wild boar and truffle – as long as it can be bought in a jar. These two items are the absolute minimum required for staving off malnutrition. You can live without olive oil, salt, pepper, etc. as long as you have these two items and some running water.

The B List

To get slightly more elaborate, you will need a few more things. These mean you will be able to make your own sauces, or ' jolly up' bought ones:

- Lemons
- Onions
- Garlic
- Eggs (free range, you really can taste the difference)
- Butter (keep it in the freezer if you do not use it very often)
- Olive oil
- Sea salt
- Black peppercorns in a mill.

With these, plus your pasta and sauce, you can make Spanish omelette (eggs with onions and potatoes); hollandaise (egg, lemon and butter); mayonnaise, garlic or plain (oil, eggs, lemon juice, garlic); pasta with jar sauce and caramelised onion; roasted garlic; lemon scrambled eggs; soufflé (pasta sauce enriched with egg yolk and fluffed up with the white).

The C List

There are a few more things that we would recommend trying to have to hand. In no particular order, these are:

- Tins of good quality chopped peeled tomatoes
- Baked beans
- Dried chilli flakes for pepping up boring stir fries
- Caster sugar (more versatile than granulated)
- Dark chocolate (the good stuff – 70% cocoa solids minimum)
- Soy sauce
- Parmesan (this can also be frozen, but it does keep very well in the refrigerator)
- Ready made curry paste (somehow less dusty tasting than curry powder)

Before You Begin

- Nutmeg (not strictly an essential but there is no substitute for its delicate spicy flavour in spinach, custards or mashed parsnips)
- Dijon mustard
- Tomato ketchup
- Worcestershire sauce (put a splash in anything made with beef – and it is delicious on avocados)
- Mango chutney
- Pesto (you can stir it into mashed potatoes, or spread it over salmon and grill it, or mix it into a salad dressing)
- Tube of tomato paste
- Red wine vinegar
- Balsamic vinegar (for the world's least elaborate salad dressing – balsamic vinegar and extra virgin olive oil; or splashed into stews to add a rich edge; or a few drops over slightly less than ripe strawberries)
- Marsala or Madeira – add a slug of something alcoholic to most dishes, and these two are the most usual and they keep for ages in a cupboard once opened without going off
- Plain flour (you can always add baking powder to transform it into self-raising)
- Flavourless oil e.g. groundnut (unless any of your guests are allergic to it) or sunflower
- Two grades of olive oil – virgin (for cooking); and extra virgin (for drizzling over cooked foods and salads, and dipping good bread into)
- Black olives
- Stock cubes
- Dried herbes de Provence (wonderful in mince)
- Vanilla essence – the real stuff please, not the grim fake version which just tastes like dusty sugar
- Dried bay leaves
- Clear honey
- Ordinary white rice (you can use basmati for almost everything these days)
- There is a fantastic 'cheat's' risotto rice available in the pasta aisle in supermarkets which is already flavoured with spinach, saffron, sun-dried tomato or squid ink, which cooks in 10 minutes – quicker than some pastas – leave it as it is or add whatever you have to hand for a more elaborate supper

- Ready cooked udon noodles (sold in individual portions) – just heat through in the soup provided and you have a quick, low-fat supper
- Large bag of Kettle Chips and a bottle of red wine (for the days when doing any form of cooking would be just too much to bear)
- Dried herbs.

Freezer

- A packet of ready rolled puff pastry (frozen – it defrosts in minutes)
- 1 sliced loaf (brown or white)
- Frozen peas
- Frozen spinach if you like it
- Parma ham or proper dry cured bacon (not the squishy supermarket stuff which oozes white curds when fried). Freeze it in pairs of rashers and it will defrost quickly
- Packet of butcher's sausages (the supermarket ones are lovely). They can, in an emergency, be cooked from frozen under the grill, as long as you make sure they are cooked and properly hot right through. Ordinary pork or Cumberland or Lincolnshire would be our advice. The more 'adventurous' combinations can be a little disappointing.

There may be a real disaster such as a power cut, or the main course may be burnt or frozen. If a major problem occurs from which your meal will not recover, you do not have any choice; admit defeat, bury your head, and offer an apology. Make do with what you have or go out, or order in.

Much depends on your guests. Many guests do not mind if something goes wrong as long as you can verify that the power cut was due to high winds. You may attempt a night light barbecue, rummage for a camping stove and make mince and mash whilst telling ghost stories. Perhaps order a curry or go out to the pub. If you live in a city then any domestic cooking problem should be met as an opportunity. In the country, however, such flexibility is a little more difficult.

Chapter 1

Breakfast

"Go to work on an egg"
(British Egg Marketing Board)

I have a friend whose wife keeps two kinds of cereal in the house: ordinary cereal and weekend cereal. Ordinary cereal is the healthy, life prolonging, mouth numbingly dull kind. I name no names, but 'muesli', 'high fibre', 'sugar free' and 'can help reduce cholestorol' will feature heavily on the packaging. Whereas weekend cereal is exciting, flavoursome, brightly coloured, E-numbery, so-sugary-you-are-hyperglycaemic-by-noon stuff that comes with thrilling toys in the packet. Breakfast increasingly amounts only to cereal, toast, or even sometimes nothing at all in the rush to get to work. Cereal bars and frozen fruit-filled toasts claim to be breakfast foods but their validity rests on their taste, nutritional content and right to exist in any form at all.

This, I'm afraid, is the whole problem with breakfast. During the week, no-one has time to make proper breakfasts. We scuttle out of the door bolting toast, or eat a croissant at our desks. Also, to be honest, it would kill us to have eggs, bacon, sausage, tomato, beans, black pudding, eggy bread, hash browns and a fried slice every morning. Goodbye arteries. But once in a while, when you have the time, a proper breakfast is simply unbeatable. And to achieve this, you need – a man. Call me old fashioned, but, like barbecues, only blokes can really cook a proper fried breakfast. All that red meat and cholesterol lying on a platter? Me man, show me fire. Stand back and let him have the frying pan. You can fluff around in the background in your negligée, making toast. And then shock him rigid when you sit down, turn your elbows up and devour like a wild beast, stoking every so often from a pint mug of tea.

The only breakfast that you will probably serve yourself is when you have house guests and breakfast is served relatively late in the morning. Generally, this will include fried food including bacon, steak, mushrooms, onions, tomatoes, eggs and potato scones coupled with the mandatory toast and tea.

Even simple cooking such as frying an egg can be delicious. Place a pan on a very low heat, melt some butter. Crack an egg and add salt and pepper as required. Cover the pan with a lid and leave to stand for about five minutes. The eggs are cooked with a wonderful buttery taste.

An alternative to the cooked fried breakfast is something containing exotic fruit such as papaya and mango. Hard Dutch or Swedish cheeses are tasty in the morning with fresh rolls. Your breakfasts can even take on a Central American influence with servings of rice, beans, egg and flour tortillas. Potato omelette (or *'tortilla'*) is best made the night before and left to cool when it may be served for breakfast or as a packed lunch; these are ideal hot or cold. Other cultures advocate the drinking of hot chocolate for breakfast.

The Working Breakfast

There seems nowadays to be a very dangerous concept going around: that of the working breakfast. I think this can only be A Bad Thing. Working breakfasts are the reserve of politicians and business types who are keen to impress someone with their ability to work at all times of the day. First thing in the morning you want to be teasing your delicate digestive system into life gradually, not brutalising it by ingesting sausage and bacon whilst discussing the terms of a massive hostile take-over with three lawyers and the development director. Don't Try This At Home. If you must talk business at breakfast, you can't cook the breakfast as well. No-one will take you seriously if you're leaping up and down in a pinny checking on the porridge. How can you discuss the forthcoming recruitment freeze with someone with her head in the oven?

If circumstances dictate that you do have to have a working breakfast at home, keep it simple. Unless you are utterly mad and enjoy rods on your own back, buy it in. All the big supermarkets have excellent pâtisserie counters, or you can go to your local baker's. Warm the muffins through in the oven by all means, but please don't do anything more complicated than that. Leave it for when you have more time to be creative. And to my mind, this means brunch.

Brunch

Now I have to admit that I find brunch a little overrated. This is probably because, irritatingly for those who are not, I am a morning person, yes, yes, I am. I leap out of bed with a glad cry to greet the morn. I do not sulk, I do not limp around the house nursing a cup of coffee for two hours before I can even speak to people, I sail forth into the day being perky and bubbly from hour zero. God, it's annoying for everyone else. So generally, by the time normal humans are surfacing, I have been up and 'in-yer-face' cheerful for hours. So brunch, with its putative 'breakfast' link, falls into that awkward time – it's three hours away from when I get up, and I know that if I don't eat before then my blood sugar level will go through the floor and I will feel sick, but I also know that if I do eat, then I won't be hungry for brunch because I've already had breakfast and I usually don't eat lunch for five hours after that. Dilemma, dilemma, and one I haven't really solved. But I do make brunch, from time to time, usually on a Sunday, and usually for friends who live nearby. Brunch is more casual than a Sunday lunch, and you should be prepared for people turning up feeling a bit ramshackle after Saturday night. This will also have a knock-on effect on punctuality. But luckily, because all real brunches start with Bloody Marys, soon you won't mind that Alan is nearly an hour late, and will even be glad, because it will give you more time to mooch through the paper. And that's another thing – get in plenty of newspapers. *The Sunday Times* is good, for sheer acreage if nothing else, and you have to have at least one sordid tabloid (if not more). I would reckon three papers as a base number and then add at will.

Brunch is definitely the sort of meal that you have to have in the kitchen – dining room is too stiff – or even better, in the garden. Again, the great trick here is to do as much as possible ahead of time, and also to make good-tempered food which won't spoil. If you've gone for the kitchen option, you could make something like pancakes, because you can talk to your guests and just keep flipping the pancakes onto their plates. Stock up the table with jams, lemon juice, sugar, butter, golden syrup, maple syrup and let them build their own combinations. Fresh fruit is yucky with pancakes – I'm sorry, nutritionists, but this is true. Honourable exception is made for Chris's mom's homemade blueberry pancakes, and even they were served with industrial quantities of crispy bacon and maple syrup. Pancakes are quite hard work for the cook, though, and you run the risk of being short-changed yourself. If you do want to make them, you can make them slightly ahead and keep them warm in a low oven covered with a slightly damp tea towel. This isn't ideal, because they can and probably will go a bit leathery, but it gets round you being chained to the cooker for the entire morning.

Kedgeree is a good option, and a classic brunch dish. It is great in that you can add and subtract at will, and don't have to have the exact quantities of each ingredient. But do use undyed smoked fish (unless you like your meals to look radioactive), and I do also think that kedgeree needs to have hard-boiled eggs. Actually smoked fish always goes down well at breakfast. I think it's something to do with strong salty flavours to wake you up, especially if you're feeling a little bit under the weather after Saturday night. (I will admit here to liking grilled Stilton on toast for mild hangover breakfasts. Or sausage and marmalade sandwiches. Sorry everyone.) You could do smoked salmon and scrambled egg (but please, don't stir the salmon into the hot egg and cook it – just snip it over the top at the last minute), or produce masses of fresh bagels and cream cheese and smoked salmon, or – if you don't mind your kitchen being a bit fishy for a while – you could grill kippers, which are delicious served with mountains of hot buttered toast and some wicked horseradish. Fishcakes are another good fishy brunch dish.

You also need something sweet and a bit 'picky' for people to dibble in while sipping the last of the coffee and mooching through the papers. Crumbly-topped, warm cinnamon and walnut cake – a typical American coffee cake – is good, or orange cornmeal muffins, or even just really good fresh scones, which are ridiculously easy. Also, if you happen to have some homemade jam kicking about, now is the time. Jam is very very easy to make, and people always forget, you don't need to make it in industrial quantities. A couple of punnets of raspberries in the summer can be set aside and boiled up with some sugar. You don't even need to be too worried about how well it sets – it's homemade, let's not forget – you can always busk it. 'Yes, this is my grandmother's recipe, isn't it wonderful how runny it is, you can see the fruit much better this way, and of course it's simply wonderful over ice cream.' Or, the opposite extreme, the jam which has set like a rubber tyre – 'mm, yes, it's lovely and firm, isn't it, it's so good on really proper thick toast' (i.e. the only way you'll get it onto bread without destroying it utterly is to make sure you've broiled the slice to the durability of granite). The most delicious jam I ever made was rosepetal jam. It was February and I was recipe testing for a book on preserves, and needed proper scented roses for this recipe (those sad little anaemic ones that smell only of cellophane would never have done.) I went to Moyses Stevens and spent nearly £70 on 17 beautiful pink blowsy roses, which yielded, when cooked, half a jar of jam. But what jam! It was like something from the Arabian nights, attar of roses, Turkish delight, and the most beautiful, deep (hideous stains on the saucepan) velvety shocking pink. I eked it out, a teaspoon at a time, on fromage blanc or stirred into organic yoghurt, for completely self-indulgent puddings. It would have been completely wrong on toast.

Bloody Marys

Kedgeree

Smoked Salmon Scrambled Eggs

Fishcakes

Cinnamon and Walnut Streusel Cake

Orange Cornmeal Muffins

Scones

Raspberry Jam

Bloody Marys
My friend Hugo gave me the best tip ever for Bloody Marys – they taste infinitely better if you add a slug of sherry. Also, they taste much better made in large jugfuls than in individual glasses.

> 250ml/8floz vodka
> 700ml/1¼ pts tomato juice
> 125ml/4floz dry sherry
> Worcestershire sauce
> Tabasco
> lemon juice
> salt and pepper (you can use celery salt, if you like, but be careful as it's quite strong tasting).

Mix and serve over ice.

Kedgeree

I have a bizarre preference for kedgeree made with brown rice. It's just one of those things, I'm afraid. Feel free to make it with white if you prefer. Again, this is a basic recipe which you can tamper with at will. Add chopped tomatoes, or currants (although frankly I think that would be an abomination), or use salmon, or leave out the eggs. It's your breakfast.

> 175g/6oz brown rice
> 500g/1lb smoked haddock fillet
> 3oz butter
> 1 onion, chopped
> 1 tbsp curry powder
> 2 hard-boiled eggs, chopped
> 3 tbsps chopped fresh parsley
> grated rind one lemon.

Poach the fish in just enough water to cover. Bring to the simmering point, then simmer for 10 minutes until just done. Drain, skin and flake. Use the water to cook the rice until tender, then drain. Fry the onion gently in the butter till softened but not browned. Add the curry powder and cook briefly. Then add the fish and rice and heat through, stirring gently so as not to break up the fish too much. Stir in the egg, parsley and lemon, check for seasoning and serve.

Smoked Salmon Scrambled Eggs

If you have your own recipe for scrambled eggs, then do please use it. This is just for those of you who may never have made it before.

Breakfast

6 eggs
60ml/2floz milk or to be devilish, cream
salt
masses of freshly ground black pepper
30g/1oz butter
4 slices smoked salmon (or you could use smoked salmon trimmings – ask your fishmonger for these scrappier – and cheaper – bits), cut into strips chopped fresh parsley and grated lemon rind to garnish (optional).

Beat together the eggs, milk and seasoning in a jug. Melt the butter in a non-stick saucepan over quite a high heat and pour in the eggs. Turn the heat down to low and stir gently with a wooden spoon till the mixture is starting to catch on the bottom. Stir and scrape the bottom of the pan, pushing off the egg in long curdy strips, till it is just slightly runnier than you would serve it (bear in mind it will carry on cooking a little bit as you serve it, from the residual heat in the egg). Divide between four plates, scatter with the smoked salmon strips, parsley and lemon rind (you may feel that parsley and lemon rind are entirely Too Much Bother so early in the morning) and serve with hot buttered granary toast.

Fishcakes

500g/1lb poached fish (salmon is good, or cod, or smoked mackerel, or even tinned tuna if you are struggling) in flakes
500g/1lb mashed potato (no butter added, if possible)
2–3 tbsps chopped fresh parsley
finely grated rind half a lemon
2 tbsps tomato ketchup (optional, but The Ivy makes its fishcakes this way)
1 tsp anchovy essence (optional).

Mix all together, check for seasoning (I usually add lots of freshly ground black pepper, and if I have some chives lurking around snip in a couple of tablespoons, and possibly some mustard or if you've used mackerel, then a tablespoon of horseradish) and form into round cakes (depending on size, this will make about six). Put in the fridge till needed. Preheat oven to 200C/Gas 6. Lightly flour the fishcakes and fry them till coloured on both sides, then bake for 10–15 minutes. If you're really not in the mood to dirty more pans, then you can simply brush them with a little oil and bake them from cold (they won't be so pretty but don't say anything and I bet nobody notices).

Cinnamon and Walnut Streusel Cake

For the cake:

>60g/2oz unsalted butter, at room temperature
>125g/4oz golden caster sugar
>pinch salt
>2 eggs
>1 tsp vanilla extract
>175g/6oz plain flour
>2 tsps baking powder
>125ml/4floz milk.

Preheat the oven to 190C/Gas 5. Oil and line a 22cm/9in deep-sided cake tin (springform, or with removable base). Cream the butter, sugar and salt till pale and fluffy; add the eggs and vanilla and beat well. Sieve the flour with the baking powder and beat in along with the milk. It will probably have curdled. Don't worry. Pour into the prepared pan and bake for 30–40 minutes till a skewer inserted in the middle comes out clean. Allow to cool in the tin.

For the topping:

>125g/4oz flaked or desiccated coconut
>60g/2oz chopped walnuts (you could of course use almonds or hazelnuts)
>60g/2oz unsalted butter, at room temperature
>90g/3oz demerara sugar
>1 tsp ground cinnamon
>2 tbsps milk.

Mix together, spread over the cooled cake and grill until browned. Cool before serving.

Breakfast

Orange Cornmeal Muffins

You can make these in individual muffin tins, but I make one large cake (for no other reason than, rather shamingly, I don't actually own any muffin tins). You don't have to use wholemeal flour –it just makes me feel a bit healthier. You could add sultanas to this, or chocolate chips (in which case, remember that healthy feeling? Kiss it goodbye), or dried cherries, or leave out the orange and flavour them with vanilla and nutmeg. I often put these together when I get up and put them into the oven while I have my shower – you leap, clean and fresh, to the breakfast table, as the oven timer rings. Suzy Homemaker or what?

> *60g/2oz self raising wholemeal flour*
> *½ tbsp baking powder*
> *½ tsp salt*
> *150g/5oz instant polenta (cornmeal)*
> *30g/1oz sugar*
> *60g/2oz butter, melted*
> *1 egg, beaten*
> *150ml/¼ pt milk (skimmed is fine)*
> *grated rind and juice one orange.*

Butter a 22cm/9in deep-sided cake tin with removable base. In a mixing bowl combine the flour, baking powder, salt, polenta and sugar. In a jug, beat the butter with the milk, eggs, rind and juice. Pour into the flour and stir just enough to mix. Pour into the cake tin and bake at 200C/Gas 6 for about 20 minutes, till golden brown. These have a really lovely gritty, grainy texture and go surprisingly well with bacon, as well as the more expected butter and marmalade.

Scones

These are surprisingly good for Sunday breakfast, even if you're not doing the full brunch monty, as they are so easy to zip together. Again, you can make them with wholemeal flour if you want to feel a bit healthier.

> *250g/8oz self raising flour*
> *60g/2oz butter at room temperature*

> 1½ tbsps caster sugar
> pinch salt
> 150ml/¼ pt milk.

Rub the butter into the flour, using your fingertips, till the mixture resembles coarse breadcrumbs. With a knife stir in the sugar and salt, then mix in the milk (don't put all of it in at once – it depends on the flour how much liquid you will need). If you are using wholemeal flour, you may need a bit more milk. When it is sticking together, squeeze it a bit with your hands to a soft dough. Plop onto a floured surface and roll it out to about 3cm/1½ in thick. Either cut into the desired shape with a sharp knife, or use a pastry cutter to cut out the scones. My house doesn't have a pastry cutter, so I use a mug. Which works perfectly as long as you push it straight down and don't twist it into the dough, because that will distort the finished scone. You can scoop up any unused dough and reform into one final scone, but be warned, it will never rise as high or be as pretty as the rest of them. You can eat that one. Another variation on the scone theme (and I would use white flour for this, not wholemeal). Add a couple of ounces of chopped dried pear before you mix in the milk, and sprinkle the dough surface with a mixture of brown sugar and dried ginger (press it in slightly before baking). Cut the scones slightly larger than usual. Yum. Put the raw scones on a baking sheet and bake for 12–15 minutes (depending on the size of the cut-outs) – they should be pale golden brown. Cool on a wire rack but eat still slightly warm, with lots of butter and raspberry jam.

Raspberry Jam

You can make this in any quantity. All you need to remember is same weight of sugar as berries.

> 500g/1lb raspberries
> 500g/1lb granulated sugar
> various jars, washed and put in a roasting tin with their lids (I have a random collection made up of pasta sauce jars, pickled onion jars, mustard pots and even jam jars, occasionally). Sorry to state the obvious but no plastic lids, please.

Put the raspberries in a heavy-based pan on a low heat, and at the same time put the sugar in a heatproof bowl into a moderate (180C/Gas 4) oven. Cook the fruit for about 30 minutes, stirring carefully up from the bottom from time to time (carefully to avoid mushing the fruit up too much), until it's all cooked and the berries are really soft and tender. Now add the hot sugar and leave on a low heat, stirring occasionally, for about 15 minutes, until the sugar has fully dissolved – this is vital. If there are any sugar crystals left, the jam will crystallise round them and go gritty. Take the roasting tin of jam jars and put in the hot oven to sterilise in the meantime. When you are sure the sugar has completely dissolved, turn the heat up as high as possible and boil hard for 10 minutes. There will be the most fantastic smell. After the 10 minutes, put a teaspoonful of jam onto a saucer – when it has cooled, push it with your finger. If it goes crinkly and a skin has formed, it has set. If not, continue to boil and test at five-minute intervals (although to be honest don't worry too much – as I said above, you can always busk it with homemade jam). Skim off any scum with a slotted spoon. I don't bother. It all adds to the authentic homemade look. Let the jam settle for about 10–15 minutes then give it a good stir and pour it into the warmed jars, filling them to the top. Cover with waxed discs and allow to cool, then put on the lids.

Chapter 2

Lunch

I am slightly wary of people who say that lunch is their favourite way to entertain. 'It's so relaxed, you have the whole day to prepare, and then the whole afternoon to clear up afterwards.' This is certainly true, but I personally am not sure that a whole day spent in the kitchen can be termed relaxing. The old adage about work expanding to fill the time available is never more true than when talking about food preparation and clearing up. It's not like a supper party, when you have consciously dedicated an evening ahead of time to work solidly at shopping and cooking. Instead of a nice leisurely morning mooching round the garden dead-heading a few roses before slicing up the cold ham, you will spend ALL morning making lunch, and then ALL afternoon clearing up, probably slightly annoyed at your guests for still being there while you are running around plying them with coffee and liqueurs and trying to scrape the remains of the casserole into the dog bowl and still thinking about what time the children have to be at the swimming pool tomorrow morning.

Because this is the other thing about lunch – unless you are retired or don't have to work, in which case no rules apply – it only happens at weekends. And it will generally happen on a Sunday, purely because on Saturday most people are running around catching up on shopping, housework, supermarket visits, taking Charles to extra maths tuition, looking at new houses, whatever. This is a bit of a shame, because Sunday Lunch is such an institution that it is very hard to break away from tradition and do anything except a roast. I know people claim roasts are the easiest things in the world, and yes, to an extent, they are, but as I point out in the chapter on having people to stay for the weekend, there is nothing more difficult than juggling the timing of three kinds of vegetables, roast potatoes and Yorkshire puddings whilst simultaneously wondering whether the crumble needs to go in now. The meat is easy – no question about that – buying a good quality chunk of protein and putting it in the oven is hardly rocket science – but the accompaniments will finish you off. So there are two kinds of lunch – the Saturday Lunch, and the Sunday Lunch.

And within these categories, just like dinner, there are sub-categories. These typically include the **Family Lunch** – and here I am not talking about days when it's you, your husband or wife plus your children. I reckon you've known them long enough not to need instructions on what to cook them. No, this kind of family lunch is when you have invited Roger's maiden aunt Jean, or you've got a godmother or two coming over because they haven't seen little Davina in ages, or your parents-in-law are dropping in on their way somewhere else.

Then there is the **Friends Lunch** – which may or may not involve children (if it does, then kindly move immediately to p. 34; otherwise stay here). Peculiarly, this is often more relaxed than having your family over. Maybe it's because you know your friends have chosen to love you, whereas you have to make more of an effort with your family as they are going to report straight back to all the cousins, your mother, Great Aunt Doris, whoever, on what a slattern you are and how you couldn't even make a white sauce that wasn't lumpy (see p. 37 for hints, by the way). Obviously some of your family are not going to be like this, so you don't have to knock yourself out trying to impress them – you can treat them as friends, and isn't that nice (and unusual).

Finally, there is the **Occasion Lunch** – somebody's birthday, or to announce an engagement. These tend to be rather grander affairs and with more people than you would normally cook for.

Saturday Lunch for friends is easy. Rustic foods: chunky soups for example or giant mixed salads in the summer, or chicken pie in the winter. If your elderly aunt has come down to the country especially then you have to make a little more effort – only a little, mind you, this is still lunch, after all, so we're not doing spun sugar cages on our puddings, I don't care who they are. You can produce some cheese afterwards if they still look hungry. For **Sunday Lunch** you are almost committed to doing a roast, and if that's what you end up doing, then I can give you no better advice than to sit down with a cookery book you trust – any of the basic *Good Housekeeping* ones, or a Delia, would be the two that I would suggest – that will give you the relative roasting times for lamb or pork, and then work out a rigid timetable. Put meat on at x time, put potatoes in at y time, start making gravy at z time. Plan it like a military operation, like those lists you see in women's magazines around Christmas time, which basically map out your entire morning in the kitchen without so much as giving you a break for a glass of sherry. It's brutal.

Now then. To be perfectly honest, having said you must do a roast on Sunday, I find the thought so daunting that I have never done so. There's hypocrisy for you. Yes, I have roasted meat – I'm particularly good at ham – but there are no massed ranks of accompanying vegetalia, there is no gravy, there is certainly no Yorkshire pudding. My Sunday lunches are usually based round hearty but elegant casseroles (like coq au vin, or lamb tagine with prunes), and then a tart or baked custard to follow. Or in the summer, a whole cold poached salmon, and then a tart to follow. Or of course, curry. And why is this? So you can get it done in advance. The roast chicken recipe I give you here is completely 'one-pot' – it incorporates its own potatoes, sauce and at least one vegetable, so you only need to worry about one other vegetable. And as I said before, if you are determined to do a proper old-fashioned Sunday roast dinner with all the trimmings, you can work out roasting times and temperatures for yourself from any of the good basic cookbooks. Just don't ask me to do it.

Lunch Invitations

Use the same 'at Home' cards as for dinner, but state 'Lunch' and give a time. You may need to give good notice for a lunch. People's weekends can become booked months in advance especially during the busy summer holiday period. If there are significant miles for your guests to travel, then allow a proportional amount of leeway in their estimated arrival time, and judge your menu and cooking accordingly.

Lunch

Friends' Lunch Suggested Menu

Roasted Yellow Pepper Soup with Feta, Mint and Tomato

Pork Marengo with Giant Oven Chips

Baked Amaretti Peaches

Roasted Yellow Pepper Soup with Feta, Mint and Tomato

>1 onion, chopped
>knob of butter
>4 yellow peppers, roasted, skinned and cut into chunks
>450ml/¾ pt stock
>pinch saffron or turmeric (for the colour)
>slab feta cheese (you won't need all of it, but it's difficult to get smaller amounts), chopped in small cubes
>1 tbsp chopped fresh mint
>2 tomatoes, skinned if you can be bothered, and chopped.

Soften the onion in the butter till going translucent, then add the peppers, stock and saffron or turmeric. Bring to the boil then simmer till the vegetables are tender (10–15 minutes). Whiz in a blender and check for seasoning. Serve in small amounts, sprinkled with the feta, mint and tomato. Depending on the time of year, this can also be served chilled. It also occurs to me that this would be another great soup to serve as a canapé in tiny espresso cups (see Chapter 7).

Pork Marengo

Like all casseroles, this improves by being made a day or two in advance. Isn't that lucky, since the chips need to be cooked at a higher temperature, and this means you can reheat the pork on the hob on the day.

>600g/1¼ lbs boneless pork, in 2cm/1in cubes
>olive oil
>2 onions, chopped
>1 tbsp flour
>1 clove garlic, crushed
>150ml/5floz dry white wine

> bay leaf
> thyme
> grated rind one orange
> 1 tin chopped tomatoes
> tomato purée.

Brown the pork in batches in the olive oil; set aside. Brown the onion in the same fat. Work in the flour; cook for one minute then stir in the garlic, wine, herbs, orange rind, tomatoes and tomato purée. Season well, bring to the boil and simmer to reduce slightly. Pour over the meat, bring back to the boil, cover and put in the oven for 1½ hours at 150C/Gas 3. Serve with giant chips (or it's also very good with plain rice), and some sort of green vegetable. Spinach, somehow, goes very well, but people tell me I am unhealthily obsessed with spinach (even to the extent of eating it cold) so you don't have to have it.

Giant Oven Chips

> 1kg/2lb potatoes, washed but not peeled
> 4 tbsps olive oil
> 3 tbsps dark soy sauce.

Preheat the oven to 190C/Gas 5. Cut the potatoes lengthways into giant chips and toss in a bowl with the oil, soy sauce and lots of black pepper. Turn onto a baking tray and bake for 40–45 minutes, turning occasionally, until brown and crisp. Children adore these.

Baked Amaretti Peaches

Another one of those recipes that is more a method than anything else, but it is so good this can be forgiven.

> 4 large peaches (you can use tinned if you must, but I think it would be better to make something else if there aren't fresh peaches about)
> 6–8 of those big Amaretti biscuits that come in the paper twists
> 60g/2oz butter, at room temperature
> ½ tsp cinnamon (optional – like spinach, it's one of my favourite things so ignore me if I use it all the time and use your own judgement)
> small glass Marsala or half Marsala, half water.

Halve the peaches and stone them. Crush the biscuits and mix to a paste with the butter and cinnamon if using. Stuff the stone cavities of the peach halves with this mixture and put face up in a baking dish. Pour the wine into the base of the dish and bake at 190C/Gas 5 for 15–20 minutes, basting once or twice. Delicious with good vanilla ice cream.

Family Lunch
Suggested Menu

Watercress Roulade with Horseradish and Smoked Trout
Creamy Chicken, Leek and Mushroom Pie
Pommes au Beurre

Watercress Roulade with Horseradish and Smoked Trout

For the roulade:

> *1 packet ready washed watercress*
> *salt, pepper and nutmeg*
> *1 tbsp full fat cream cheese (from the packet you use later)*
> *3 eggs, separated.*

Line a swiss roll tin with silicon paper and put the oven on to 180C/Gas 4. Cover the watercress with the seasoning, cheese and egg yolks. Stiffly whip the whites and fold the two together. Turn into the tin and bake for about 15 minutes. It will be all puffed up and then it will collapse. Don't worry, this is normal. Turn out onto a clean tea towel over a wire rack and cover with another tea towel. Allow to cool.

For the filling:

> *2 smoked trout fillets, flaked*
> *another packet watercress, one half chopped, one half left whole*
> *half a packet cream cheese (or more, or less, depending)*
> *1–2 tbsps horseradish*
> *salt and pepper.*

Mash the trout with the chopped watercress, cream cheese, salt, pepper and horseradish to taste. If it is very stiff, slacken it with some mayonnaise or in an utter crisis a tablespoon of milk to make it of a spreading consistency. Lift the tea towel off the roulade and peel the silicon paper off its underneath. Spread the trout mixture over the underneath and roll up, using the tea towel underneath it to help you. This makes rather more than four people need, but it is harder to make less. Serve garnished with the remaining watercress.

Creamy Chicken, Leek and Mushroom Pie

> 1 large chicken (The most economical way to do this is roast the chicken yourself, cool it and strip off the flesh and then use the bones to make the stock – but this does mean quite a lot of planning ahead. More often I just buy one of those freshly cooked supermarket chickens and make up a stock cube, or see if I've got any stock in the freezer.)
> 90g/3oz butter
> 1 onion, chopped
> 3 large leeks, sliced
> 1 tsp curry powder
> 60g/2oz plain flour
> 500ml/1pt milk
> 300ml/$^1/_2$ pint chicken stock
> 2–3 tbsps mascarpone
> 2 tbsps chopped parsley
> 250g/$^1/_2$ lb (or more, to taste) mushrooms, sliced
> 350g/12oz packet puff pastry (and these days I buy the ready rolled stuff).

Fry the onion and leek in the butter till translucent. Stir in the curry powder and flour; cook for 1–2 minutes, then add the milk and stock and stir until boiling. Season well. Take off the heat, stir in the mascarpone, mushrooms, chicken and parsley. If you like, you can add a dash of dry sherry at this stage. Don't worry that the mushrooms haven't been cooked – they will cook in the time the pie is in the oven. Put into a pie dish, cover with the pastry (use the trimmings to make decorative leaves and what not, if you like), brush with beaten egg and bake at 220C/Gas 7 for the first 20 minutes, then turn the heat down to 180C/Gas 4 for a further 20 minutes. This is quite a good one to have up your sleeve at Christmas time because if you've massively misjudged the size of your turkey, this is an ideal way to use up the leftovers. Good served with carrots (colour contrast) and plain boiled new potatoes.

Pommes au Beurre

This is based on a very old English recipe of Eliza Acton's.

> 6 eating apples
> 90g/3oz unsalted butter, cubed
> 90g/3oz caster sugar
> 1 tsp cinnamon
> 4 tbsps apricot jam.

Peel and core the apples (do not cut them in half). Put the apples in a saucepan just large enough to hold them, and strew the butter over. Place on a very low heat and when the butter has melted, cover and stew very gently for about half an hour until nearly done, turning the apples carefully from time to time so they cook evenly. (You can do this ahead, up to this point, in which case cook the apples for perhaps 5 minutes less than you think they'll need.)

Mix the sugar and cinnamon and sprinkle over the apples, and turn up the heat so the sauce boils and goes butterscotchy (about 5 minutes). In a separate pan warm up the jam. Put the apples into a serving dish, cavity uppermost, and pour a little jam into each one. Pour the butterscotch sauce over and around the apples and serve with really cold vanilla ice cream.

Traditional Sunday Lunch

The roast joint of beef, lamb or pork is a great institution, albeit an impossible one for the vegetarian. For centuries, it has survived shoddy cooking in homes and taverns up and down the country. The real secret of a good roast lunch is to successfully comprehend how to pack as much food on the plate as possible, and to cover it in gravy without the food and gravy falling off the side of it. A few *faux pas* when cooking a traditional lunch:

- overcooking green vegetables
- serving watery mash
- failing to mix up the packet gravy to the extent that it becomes lumpy
- serving unadventurous accompaniments, your three vegetables should not consist of chips, mash and roast
- failing to provide condiments, horseradish, mint, apple, cranberry, etc.

A proper roast lunch requires no starter course. If you are hungry afterwards then remember to cook more next time. There is considerable debate over the acceptability of frozen Yorkshire puddings. A mix of flour, egg, water, seasoning and hot oil, should not be beyond us. Practice until you can make Yorkshire pudding in your sleep. Let the world praise your Yorkshires.

The tricky bit about Yorkshire puddings is that they need to be cooked at a temperature much higher than that needed to roast meat. This means that you can't cook the two together, since either your Yorkshires will be flabby, or your meat will be incinerated. What you can do, however, is blast the puddings at 'surface of the sun' temperature while the meat is resting before you carve it. Yes, I'm sorry, it's another thing to be done at the last minute and this will contribute to your early nervous breakdown. You can either cook the puddings in individual portions in little bun tins, or as one giant whole in a rectangular enamel dish. Personally I prefer the latter, as I like the softer bits, and with the singular ones there is far too much crispy edge, but it's up to you. Just remember to reduce the cooking time for the individual ones. Whichever you do, just be sure you make enough. And cook them on the top shelf of the oven – even in a fan oven this seems to make a difference.

Yorkshire Pudding

300ml/10floz full fat milk (Look, you're about to feed your loved ones beef, roasted parsnips, buttered cabbage, gravy and roast potatoes. Now is not the time to worry about percentage butterfat in milk.)
good $\frac{1}{2}$ tsp salt

> 4 eggs
> 250g/8oz plain flour.

Make the crucial pan decision, and whichever you choose, put a bit of appropriate fat in the bottom (by this I mean dripping if you have it, flavourless oil if not) and put in a seriously hot oven (220C/Gas 7) to heat through and melt. Meanwhile, buzz the milk, salt and eggs together and then whisk in the flour. Pour the batter into the prepared tin and bake for 20 minutes (if you're making one large one, more like 10–15 if you're making the individual ones) till risen and golden.

Sunday Lunch Suggested Menu
Quick Spinach Soup
Chicken Roasted with Tomatoes, Potatoes and Olives
Pineapple Custard Tart

Quick Spinach Soup

This could just as easily be watercress soup – just amend the vegetable. The method stays the same. You have to make this at the last minute for it to keep its brilliant green colour, as if the spinach hangs around too long it goes a bit grey. It's not a problem, though – you can get the stock and potato mixture ready well in advance.

> 1 onion, finely chopped
> 2 potatoes, peeled and chopped
> knob butter
> 750ml/1½ pints light chicken stock
> pinch of nutmeg
> 1 pillow bag ready to cook baby spinach
> 300ml/½ pint whipping cream (less rich than double, but do use double if you like).

Sweat the onion and potato in the butter till softened, then add the chicken stock and a pinch of nutmeg and simmer till very tender. Season with lots of black pepper and some salt, put through the blender and set aside till needed (don't bother to wash the blender as you'll use it later). When you are ready to serve the soup, bring it back up to the boil and tip in the bag of spinach. When it has gone limp and bright green, buzz it quickly in the blender with the cream until the desired consistency. Check for seasoning and serve immediately.

Chicken Roasted with Tomatoes, Potatoes and Olives

This recipe came about because Jules and Chris gave me a chicken brick for my birthday, and I was trying to think of something more interesting than plain naked roast chicken to do with it. So if you have a chicken brick, do use it for this, but it is equally delicious just roasted normally. Good with courgettes, steamed then tossed in a little pesto, or with plain broccoli.

> *1 chicken*
> *3 cloves garlic*
> *3 tbsps olive oil*
> *juice 1 lemon*
> *500g/1lb small potatoes, halved lengthways*
> *8 plum tomatoes, halved lengthways*
> *18–25 (a big handful, for heaven's sake) Kalamata or other brine-cured olives, pitted if you can be bothered*
> *1 tbsp capers (salted, not the ones in brine) – optional – some people just do hate them, I know*
> *couple of sprigs fresh rosemary.*

Mash the garlic and mix it with the olive oil and lemon juice. Toss the potatoes, tomatoes, olives, capers if using them, and rosemary in the garlic mixture and then drain off the excess liquid. Put the vegetables in a roasting tin. Put the squeezed lemon up the chicken's backside, then park the chicken on top and pour the reserved marinade over. Roast at 220C/Gas 7 for 15 minutes per pound, until the juices run clear when tested with a sharp knife.

Pineapple Custard Tart

This is such a brilliantly retro pudding, it's fantastic.

For the sweet shortcrust pastry:

> *175g/6oz unsalted butter, at room temperature*
> *60g/2oz icing sugar*

Lunch

good pinch salt
2 egg yolks
250g/8oz plain flour.

Whiz the butter, sugar, salt and egg yolks in a food processor, then add the flour and work to a sticky mass. Chill for 30 minutes in the fridge, wrapped in clingfilm. You can try rolling it out, but I have always found it just as easy to pat it into the tin by hand – this also means you can get it really thin. You will probably have some pastry left over. Either make four biscuits with it (which is what I usually do – cook's perk), or throw it away. Prick the case with a fork and bake blind. I don't bother with baking beans these days, Philistine that I am. I find it means the base stays crisper. Just keep an eye on it as it cooks. The edges might wilt slightly and want a bit of shoring up. Now is the time you wish you hadn't made biscuits out of the extra pastry.

For the filling:

1 medium sized fresh pineapple
2–3 tbsps semolina flour or ground almonds
1 egg
1 tbsp caster sugar
90ml/3floz double cream
4 tbsps apricot jam.

Peel and core the pineapple and slice into pieces not more than ½ cm/¼ in thick. You can make them long and thin, from the full length of the pineapple, or you can cut the pineapple across into rings – whichever you prefer. Lie the slices on kitchen paper and blot them very, very thoroughly. Set the oven to 180C/Gas 4. Beat together the egg, sugar and cream. Sprinkle the base of the tart case with the semolina or ground almonds (this helps to soak up the pineapple juice so the pastry stays crisper) and arrange the pineapple slices over the base. Pour the custard carefully into the pastry case, trying as best you can not to let it flood over the top of the pineapple. If it does, don't worry, pretend it was supposed to happen. You may have some custard left over. Bake for 30–40 minutes till the custard is set. Brush any exposed pineapple with warmed apricot jam.

The **Celebration Lunch** is different. This can be for a birthday, or an engagement – oh for heaven's sake, I don't really need to explain the concept, do I? It's a bit like doing a dinner party, I suppose, but it'll be less pressurised. You hope. You can go two routes here: (a) the kilt-burster – feed them all so full that they lie around like elephant seals after lunch and go home to a light supper of two Rennies and a glass of milk; or (b) feed them delicious, tasty, but ultimately life-enhancing food so they can continue to talk to one another in a pleasant, civilised fashion for the rest of the afternoon. Or of course option (c) which I neglected to mention, which is kind of a combination of the two: feed them light food but make it just so delicious that they can't resist having way too much of it. I think cooking a whole fish for this sort of lunch is perfect – it looks spectacular and it's actually not very much trouble. Also, this is a good sort of interseasonal meal. If it turns out scorchingly hot, serve the salmon cold and precede it with something like artichokes vinaigrette. Yes, they are deeply messy to eat, but you are celebrating – presumably with friends, so why are you worried? If it turns out to be teeming down rain or hail, then hey presto, hot salmon and something warm and tomatoey, soup maybe, or the tomato tart from p. 137.

Business and Working Lunches

It is unlikely, though not impossible, that you will be entertaining at lunch time in your home on a workday. You may live near your office, or work freelance from home. Entertaining at a restaurant or bar might be inappropriate for particular guests. If so, then consider the following tips:

- Keep the food light and do not drink too much wine
- Consider salads, no more than two courses and serve plenty of mineral water
- Returning to work, either asleep, drunk or both is not good. A walk back to work may revive you
- If returning to work is less pressured than it might be, then enjoy your freedom to entertain at a more relaxed pace.

Weekend Lunches

The weekend lunch is a much more enjoyable affair. These can be an excellent excuse to start drinking Bloody Mary's at 11.30 a.m., as you begin to prepare the food. It might be desirable to plan an activity after lunch, such as a walk, a game of croquet or perhaps something like petanque. This rounds off the event, and may even improve digestion.

Saturday lunch is not a time for elaborate menus. A rule of thumb is to serve lighter food and less alcohol than at later events in the day. There is no need for five different wines and the ubiquitous port glasses. It is fine to serve soup, but then many feel that if the soup is good it is satisfactory to serve it at any time. You should always keep a large quantity of gazpacho on tap. Do not use candlesticks for lunch, unless you are lunching in an Arctic winter, where darkness rules and etiquette comes a poor second to the need to see. Use flowers to decorate a table. Try to use the prettier of your sets of china and ensure that everything that is supposed to sparkle does so. Under the harsh light of day, smeared and tarnished metal looks decidedly tatty.

Suggested Menu

Plain Grilled Chicken with Salsa Verde

Cumin Roasted Carrots

Courgette Confetti

Chocolate Pavlova

Plain Grilled Chicken with Salsa Verde

> 4 skinless chicken breasts
> grated rind and juice 2 lemons
> 60ml/2floz olive oil
> chopped fresh thyme.

Marinate the chicken for as long as possible in the lemon, oil and thyme. Or indeed any other marinade you fancy. Get a heavy cast iron grill pan really hot. Wipe the excess marinade off the chicken and slam it down onto the grill pan. Cook for 6–8 minutes each side. Let rest for about 2 minutes before serving with salsa verde handed separately.

Salsa Verde

Salsa Verde has become deeply groovy. Very River Café.

Quantities given below are guidelines only. If you like more or less of a thing, add more or less of it.

>2 tbsps seriously good olive oil
>1 tbsp red wine vinegar
>2 tsps grainy mustard
>1 tsp red chilli flakes or some Tabasco
>3 tbsps chopped fresh flatleaf parsley
>2 tbsps chopped fresh mint
>2 tbsps chopped fresh basil
>1 tbsp chopped salted capers (NOT capers in brine or vinegar)
>2–3 anchovy fillets, finely chopped
>3–4 small gherkins, chopped.

Mix. Chill till needed (not longer than a couple of hours, though, as the herbs go a bit grey because of the acid in the vinegar). How easy was that? This is delicious not only with the chicken as mentioned, but also with plain grilled fish and cold roasted beef. I served it recently with beef and because it was a hot evening didn't do the roast potatoes and steamed vegetables, but instead produced plain boiled baby new potatoes and a huge salad of chicory, orange slices and red onion, which worked brilliantly.

Cumin Roasted Carrots

>6–8 large fat carrots, peeled and in fat chunks
>1 whole head garlic cloves (unpeeled)
>1 tsp cumin seeds
>1 tbsp olive oil
>salt and pepper.

Mix together – you'll be amazed that so little oil will cover everything, but it does – and roast at 190C/Gas 5 for 35–45 minutes till the carrots are slightly shrivelled and caramelised.

Courgette Confetti

>6–8 fine fat courgettes, washed, topped and tailed.

Run a potato peeler down each courgette to make ribbons. Put the whole tangle into a steamer basket over boiling water and steam for about 4–5 minutes till bright green. Sprinkle with salt and lemon juice before serving.

Chocolate Pavlova

Easy rule of thumb for making meringues – double the amount of sugar (in ounces) to egg whites. And although it is high in sugar, meringue is low in fat. I cannot, of course, make the same claim for the double cream. But you could substitute natural or Greek yoghurt, or low fat fromage frais for some if not all of the cream.

For the meringue:

> *4 large egg whites (make mayonnaise with the yolks)*
> *250g/8oz caster sugar*
> *splash vanilla*
> *1tsp malt vinegar*
> *1tsp cornflour*
> *1tsp cocoa powder.*

Turn oven to 140C/Gas 1. Whisk egg whites in a food processor with a pinch of salt till very stiff and dry. Very very gradually, beat in the sugar, a spoonful at a time, till it is thick and glossy. Stir in the vanilla, vinegar, cornflour and cocoa. Line a baking sheet with silicon paper and pile the meringue into a rough circle with slightly built-up sides. Bake for one hour until brittle, and just beginning to colour.

For the filling:

> *300ml/10floz double cream*
> *90g/3oz (approx) dark chocolate, finely grated*
> *fresh fruit – raspberries, bananas, kiwi fruit, all are good here*
> *cocoa powder for dusting*
> *chocolate fudge sauce if you really want to make them ill or diabetic.*

Whip the double cream and fold in the grated chocolate. Pile into the well and scatter with fruit. Dust with cocoa powder if liked (I'm not convinced that I do) and trickle with chocolate fudge sauce for the truly decadent. Dieters can pick off the fruit and look wistfully at the cream.

Inviting Children to Lunch

If you've got a family then you've doubtless worked out how to keep the hordes happy, but those of us with none of our own who are faced with feeding visiting godchildren, nieces and nephews can get confused. Keep it simple and unadventurous, otherwise your little guests will make their displeasure known – unusual the child who says 'yum, has this got capers in it?' This is one instance where there is really no point in trying to make food to impress. The children will spit it out in scenes akin to those in *The Exorcist*, and everyone will become harrassed and possibly tearful, and this includes the mothers as well as the children. Bear two things in mind:

1. First of all, most people with children are happy that you have even invited them and their brood over. The adults get a chance to return to a world that is for most of them (unless your friends are architects) now only a distant memory, where cream sofas and slate floors are a reality. They can indulge in glorious *schadenfreude* as they watch their little loves crayoning somebody else's wall for a change.
2. Secondly, the fact is, everybody loves nursery food. Show me a man who doesn't like treacle sponge pudding and I will show you a liar. Most people these days exist on a steady diet of Thai green curry and roasted vegetable couscous. I have seen grown men voluntarily propose marriage when faced with homemade fish pie. With peas. Or mince round.

If you are not prepared to compromise your foodie reputation by 'dumbing down' for children, then you can of course take the second option, which is to make food which is intrinsically simple, and then add interesting sauces, garnishes or vegetables to it to smarten it up for the adults. Grilled lamb chops, for example, which can be given to children neat for them to smother in tomato ketchup, and which you can serve to adults with a spritely coriander salsa, or a couple of dollops of chickpeas roughly puréed with rosemary and garlic. Or roast a chicken, and serve it with roasted fennel and shallots, or a mouth-zinging gremolata of lemon, garlic and parsley. With any luck you'll find that when the children see the adults round the table getting stuck into Turkish walnut sauce,

Lunch

they'll want to try it too, and hey presto, gastro child is born. Or not. You can do the same with puddings. Make a chocolate roulade, for example, and fill it with cream and Nutella (tell your grown up friends it's ganache, and tell the children secretly it's really Nutella. They'll be your friends for ever.)

You will also have to take a view on how you choose to entertain the children. Because like it or not, this meal will turn out to be slightly dominated by the children. They will be the focus of the attention. I am going to make a massive assumption and say that this is going to be a lunch party. It is probably unlikely that you will have seven year olds round for dinner. You will have to choose whether you are going to childproof your house beforehand to whatever extent your house is capable of being childproofed, or whether you are going to leave them to run amok amongst your prized collection of small crystal animals and play dress up with your Jimmy Choos. Again, this will depend on the ages of the children and your friends' take on discipline, and the available space for them to run around in. You can always try bribing them by getting them to 'help you in the kitchen' i.e. let them make very delicious biscuits, which yes, will decimate your kitchen, but which will give you 15 minutes precious silence the other end to talk to your friends whilst their children are gobbling said biscuits (what you haven't told your friends is that these biscuits have the highest sugar content known to man, so their journey home with little Tamara having a sugar rush will be indescribable).

It is difficult to generalise about how children will behave out of their own home environment. They will either launch into trying everything in sight, in a sort of heads down voracious locust-type style of grabbing food with their bare hands and shovelling it in, or will steadfastly refuse to allow anything past their lips that hasn't been tried and tested a thousand times at home first, and possibly not even then. Also, most children are lazy eaters, and prefer to eat small, dinky bits of food that keep their attention, rather than whole pieces of bread or steak (which is difficult and boring to chew if you are three). There is the school of thought which says take the path of least resistance when dealing with children – feed them things you know they'll eat, and let their parents worry about the nutritional aspects later. I am a great advocate of this. If little Bertie is going to throw a wobbler if faced with macaroni cheese with bacon (which is a shame, because it is very good and he'd like it), then let him eat chocolate cake. If Emily has a thing about not eating green beans, then now is the time to produce Petits Filous. Let's keep things in perspective. Children are hardy. There is a seven year old in Sunderland who has existed on nothing but white sliced loaf and strawberry jam since he was three years old. I'm not saying he'll have the best teeth in the world, but he's survived this far.

And finally, always keep a packet of fish fingers in the freezer. Grilled and stuck between two pieces of buttered white plastic bread, with tomato ketchup on the side, the fish finger sandwich has been the mainstay of many a child's diet when at my house. (They're not bad, either, when everyone else has gone home and you are lying limply on the sofa too worn out to think about supper.) I remember once reading in one of those pretentious foodie magazines that fish fingers were the new sushi. 'Strip them of their breadcrumb coating and sear them quickly in a hot pan in peanut oil, so they are charred on the outside while the inside remains chilled and almost still frozen. A divine contrast in texture and flavour.' I am not making this up. 'Strip them of their breadcrumb coating'? I mean, what nonsense is this? The breadcrumbs are the entire POINT of the fishfinger. I suppose they'll be telling us which wine to serve with them next.

Suggested Menu

Fish Pie with Peas
Mince Round
Macaroni Cheese with Bacon
Fruit Cobbler
Chocolate Swiss Roll with Nutella
Peanut Butter Cookies

Fish Pie with Peas

Not really a recipe, more a reminder of the delicious things you can put into fish pies. Word of warning though – don't add mushrooms. They always, always leak into the sauce and

Lunch

make it go grey, and you will never get a child to eat grey food.

> *170ml/6floz milk*
> *bay leaf*
> *500g/1lb haddock fillet – or cod, or salmon. Or you can use a mixture of smoked cod and fresh*
> *90g/3oz butter*
> *60g/2oz plain flour*
> *large slug cream (if you like)*
> *2 tbsps chopped fresh dill, or parsley*
> *tsp curry powder (if you use parsley) or slug dry sherry (if you use the dill)*
> *1–2 tbsps Dijon mustard, if you don't fancy either curry or sherry*
> *salt, pepper, nutmeg*
> *250g/½ lb fat prawns, peeled*
> *2–3 hard-boiled eggs, halved (optional)*
> *3–4 firm tomatoes, halved (optional)*
> *mashed potatoes made with about 500g/1lb potatoes, not too runny.*

Poach the fish in the milk with the bayleaf (err on the side of under rather than overcooking it); skin, drain and flake (reserving the milk). Make a white sauce with the butter, flour and fish poaching milk. What do you mean, you don't know how. Oh honestly. Did none of you do home economics? There are two schools of thought for the white sauce. Traditional school says, melt butter in pan, fry flour till it just starts to turn colour, then add milk a little at a time whisking it in well each time. Simmer for 2–3 minutes and that's it. School B says, put it all in a pan, bring to the boil, whisk like mad, and cook for 10 minutes till the flour stops tasting raw. Whichever way you go, the crucial word is whisk. White Sauce Goes Lumpy. This is nothing that can't be fixed by ferocious beating with a balloon whisk, so don't worry about it.

Anyway. You've got your white sauce, by whatever technique. Stir in the cream, herb of choice and curry powder or sherry or mustard. Or any combination thereof, really, as long as it tastes good to you. Season with salt, pepper and nutmeg. Carefully mix the fish, prawns, eggs and tomatoes (if using) into the white sauce and pour or spoon into the bottom of a buttered ovenproof dish. Top with the mashed potatoes, spreading them evenly across the surface of the fish and making an attractive pattern with a fork (a good tip is, if you're making this for children, to section off a bit for them and let them decorate it themselves, or draw their initials on it). Bake for 40–45 minutes at 180C/Gas 4 till the top is golden and crusty and the middle is bubbling hot. Serve with peas.

Mince Round

> 1 quantity ready rolled puff pastry
> 960g/2lb steak mince – this amount makes a nice fatly filled pie with extra gravy. You certainly don't have to use it all, you can put some in the freezer for a rainy day to have mince and tatties with later
> 2 onions, very finely chopped
> sunflower oil or other flavourless oil
> 1 stock cube or teaspoon of Marmite
> salt, pepper, Worcestershire sauce.

Traditionally mince round is made on an old, scarred, cloudy with age Pyrex pie plate. I couldn't swear that it would taste the same made in a Conran shop Japanese style cooking vessel. I suspect not.

Fry the onion in the sunflower oil till soft but not brown, then add the mince and turn the heat up to high. Cook till it's no longer raw-looking, then add a bit of water, the stock cube, seasoning and simmer for 30 minutes until thick. It should still have quite a lot of juice though. One thing – after my caveat about grey food, I will tell you now that it will probably never go really brown, this mince, unless you adulterate it with Bisto (and there are worse things you could do – follow the instructions carefully though or you will end up with a sort of dark brown lump of slime like something from a horror film, which will not dissolve). Meanwhile, line the Pyrex pie dish with one half of the pastry. Drain off the more solid mince with a slotted spoon, and use to fill the pie, stopping short of the edges. Dip your finger in water and run it round the rim of the pastry. Top with the other half of the pastry, and press down well with a fork on the damp pastry to seal. Run a sharp knife round the edge to carve off any excess pastry (you

Lunch

can make decorative leaves etc. with the trimmings, if you like, or see the tip above about putting kids' initials on the pie). Slash two holes in the top to let the steam out, brush with beaten egg and bake at 190C/Gas 5 till the pastry is golden brown and crispy. Heat up the saved mince juice which will still have quite a lot of mince floating in it, and serve as gravy. This must, must be accompanied with baked beans, plain boiled potatoes, and brown sauce (or *à la limite*, tomato ketchup).

Macaroni Cheese with Bacon

>250g/8oz pasta shapes (but traditional macaroni really is the best)
>90g/3oz plain flour
>90g/3oz butter
>900ml/1½ pints milk
>nutmeg, Dijon mustard, salt and pepper
>250g/8oz strong cheese, grated (Cheddar, Gruyère, Emmenthal, or any mixture)
>slug double cream if liked
>8–12 rashers streaky bacon, grilled till crispy.

Cook the pasta in boiling salted water for a couple of minutes less than recommended on the packet. Drain. Meanwhile, make a white sauce (see p. 37), season with nutmeg, mustard, salt and pepper and work in 150g/5oz of cheese. Add the double cream, if using, and crumble in the bacon. Try not to eat too much of it. This is your children's supper. Mix the pasta into the cheese sauce. You can also add at this stage a gratuitous vegetable – cooked chopped spinach, small cooked broccoli florets, small cubes of red pepper – if you want to make them hate you forever. Pour into a buttered baking dish, sprinkle with the rest of the cheese and bake for 25–30 minutes at 200C/Gas 6 until golden brown and bubbling.

Fruit Cobbler

This is like an American crumble – the topping is more like a scone mix.

>1kg/2lbs mixed fruit – peaches, plums, apricots, cherries, apples or any combination, in chunks

> 90g/3oz sugar (or more, or less, depending on the fruit)
> zest of 1 orange
> 1 tsp cinnamon.

Toss all together and put in the base of a lightly buttered ovenproof ceramic or glass dish.

For the topping:

> 175g/6oz self raising flour
> pinch salt
> 90g/3oz sugar
> 30g/1oz ground almonds
> 90g/3oz butter
> 2 eggs
> 250ml/8floz milk
> 1 tsp vanilla extract.

Combine the flour, salt, sugar and almonds in a bowl, and cut in the butter with a knife until coarse lumps are formed. In a jug whisk the eggs, milk and vanilla, and stir briskly into the flour mixture. Spoon over the fruit (it doesn't matter if there are gaps, it will close up) and bake for 30 minutes at 180C/Gas 4 till golden brown and firm to the touch. Serve warm or at room temperature with ice cream or custard.

Chocolate Swiss Roll with Nutella

(serves 4 greedy or 6 not greedy people)

> 50g/1$\frac{1}{2}$oz self raising flour
> pinch salt
> 2 level tbsps cocoa powder
> 2 level tbsps baking powder
> 2 eggs
> 125g/4 oz caster sugar
> 2 dessertsps lukewarm water
> 300ml/10 fl oz double cream
> 4–6 (or more – depending on how much you like it) tbsps Nutella
> fresh strawberries or raspberries.

Preheat the oven to Gas Mark 6. Base-line a swiss roll tin or baking tray with silicon paper and brush with flavourless oil (e.g. sunflower, groundnut) or melted butter. Sift together the flour, salt, cocoa powder and baking powder into bowl. In a separate bowl, lightly whisk the eggs together till just combined, then add the sugar and whisk briskly for about 5 minutes until pale and slightly fluffy and thickened. (The exact timing will depend on whether you are beating by hand or using an electric mixer.) Tip in the flour mixture and the water, and fold all together quickly, using a metal spoon. Pour into prepared tin and bake for 12–15 minutes till puffy and risen.

Cool in tin (it will shrink and wrinkle a bit), then when completely cold turn out onto a sheet of greaseproof or tinfoil (this is just to help with the rolling up) and remove paper from the base. Beat the cream till fairly stiff but not grainy and spread over the sponge, leaving about an inch clear at the sides. Now for the Nutella. You may need to warm the jar slightly to loosen the goo, either on low in the microwave (make sure you've removed all traces of the metallic paper seal), or in a basin of warm water. Or you can just put great lumps of Nutella in chunks over the cream. Believe me, no-one will complain. If you know your little guests are fond of fruit, then scatter the raspberries or slices of strawberry over the Nutella; otherwise, put them in a bowl to serve alongside later. (Also, if you are going to freeze it, I wouldn't necessarily use strawberries, as they go a bit slimy when defrosted. If you've sliced them it's not such a disaster, but if you've left them fairly whole then it could be unpleasant. Your call.) Roll up the long side of the sponge, using the foil or paper to help you. If you have made this ahead to freeze it, freeze it still wrapped in the paper. To serve, remove the paper, trim off the ends of the roulade, and dredge with icing sugar. (Thanks to Sharon Manchè for this.)

Peanut Butter Cookies
For heaven's sake, MAKE SURE that nobody has a nut allergy.

> *6 dessertspoonfuls peanut butter (crunchy or smooth, this is not an exact science)*
> *a large tin of condensed milk*
> *175g/6oz chopped roasted peanuts (NOT dry roasted)*

*125g/4oz (or more!) smashed up milk or plain chocolate
125g/4oz chopped pitted dates.*

Preheat oven to 200C/Gas 6 and line a couple of baking trays with silicon paper (you can give your Blue Peter lecture about snub-nosed scissors here). Mix all ingredients together, and using a teaspoon blob in small balls on the trays. They spread out a bit, but not too much. Bake 10–15 minutes until golden. Cool on a wire rack (if you can wait that long). Eat and pass out.

Chapter 3

Tea

The Meal

Do not feel that you have to be Bertie Wooster, a cricketing wife or an Oxford Don to enjoy tea. Many believe that tea is the best meal of the day. Tea is a meal that is less popular as a formal event than it has been, but can be an efficient way of offering hospitality to a large number of people, certainly at less cost than an evening dinner party. It can be delightful after a long weekend walk.

A high tea is a wonderfully substantial meal consisting of scones, sandwiches, cooked delicacies, different cakes, biscuits, crumpets, toasted buns. Younger children may like tea before going to an early bed.

There are really two kinds of tea. There is the tea that you have when you haven't seen a friend in ages, the only free time you both have is a Sunday afternoon, and you invite them round. Really, what will happen is that you now have an excuse to gossip like fiends for two hours, denigrating your entire social set and their hangers on, and hopefully their wardrobes as well. For this, tea itself is entirely secondary. You may provide a packet of bought chocolate chip cookies, but the tea is not the point here. Actually, to be honest, my particular favourite for this kind of tea is not to have tea at all, but to crack into a bottle of port or better yet Madeira, which is suprisingly delicious at about 5 o'clock in the afternoon. If you feel you must have something to eat, the humble digestive biscuit is sadly underrated, and also widely available on a Sunday afternoon.

The other kind of tea is Old Fashioned Country House Tea (degraded in small market towns throughout the land as Cream Tea, or in cases of particular unpleasantness, Ye Olde

Cornishe Clotted Cream Tea. This is clearly an abomination, and something to be avoided.) This kind of tea is a bit more organised and I tend to have it on a Sunday afternoon when old friends I haven't seen in a while are in town. I usually invite several people. It is altogether more substantial, involving savoury things and cakes as well as biscuits, and takes quite a lot of work beforehand. The good part is that, being a weekend, you normally have some time in which to tackle it. It also depends on the time of year as to what you decide to make: the good old cucumber sandwich is ideal for summer months, but in the winter I would suggest smoked mackerel pâté and hot brown toast. Don't listen to people who say you must have real white bread for making cucumber sandwiches: this is a fallacy put about by food snobs. Plastic bread is brilliantly squadgy against the crisp cucumber. You must cut the crusts off after you've made the sandwiches, though, and they must be made with butter not margarine or olive oil spread. Hot buttered muffins, scones with jam, chocolate chip cookies, banana bread and brownies, either bought or made, are all year round staples for tea. I am also keen on warm potato scones with butter, but then I'm Scottish.

The other thing about organized teas is that you have to have a cake. It needn't be a complicated multilayer cream-sodden one (and in fact it's probably better if it's not) but it has to be homemade. Trust me. You will not believe the plaudits you will get for making a cake. (OK – at a pinch, I will allow you to buy it from the WI or the local farm shop, but it has to have the authentic home-made slightly bashed and craggy look.) The great debate is: chocolate cake or Victoria sponge? I say neither, and usually make my mother's legendary and lethal Whisky Cake.

The other problem with big teas is that, unless you live on a working farm or are heavily involved with the local cricket team, you will only have one kettle – and trying to keep 10 people in tea is very tricky. You will have tea 'longeurs'. No way round it, unless you want to boil water in a saucepan as well (I've never been that desperate). After all, these are friends of yours you've invited round – they'll understand. And anyway, if they're anything like my friends, you'll have barged into the port (see above) at an early stage, so quantities of hot tea are less crucial. I also have no truck with people who like lemon slices in their tea. (Sorry, Dad.)

Smoked Mackerel Pâté
(for four, assuming you are feeding them other things too)

Actually I can't believe you need a recipe for this. Put one of those small packets of cream cheese in a bowl (use the low-fat stuff – you really can't taste the difference). Take the skin off a pair of smoked mackerel fillets (the ones sold under plastic in your supermarket are fine) and add to the bowl. Add a tablespoon or so of horseradish (from a jar) and a good tablespoon or so of lemon juice. If your mackerel wasn't the peppered kind, add a lot of ground black pepper. Add a tablespoon of whisky too, if you like. Now, using a pair of forks, shred the mackerel fillets and mix them together with the other ingredients. Keep stirring and shredding and mashing until it reaches your favourite consistency. I like it when there are still quite big flakes of fish left in. Cover and set aside till needed (I think this is nicest not straight from the fridge, so if you'll be eating it relatively soon leave it out of the fridge, but it can be made a couple of days in advance, in which case it will need to be kept cold). Have some extra lemon juice handy with your hot brown toast when you serve it. It shouldn't need butter but you can guarantee there are those who will demand it.

Banana Bread
(makes one 16×10.5cm/6.5×4in loaf)
This is truly delicious and could not be easier.

> *2–3 very ripe bananas (they must be really spotted with black and making your entire kitchen smell of banana)*
> *60g/2oz softened butter or margarine*
> *60g/2oz soft brown sugar*
> *½ tsp vanilla essence*
> *1 egg*
> *150g/5oz self raising flour (you can use white or wholemeal, depending on how virtuous you feel)*
> *¼ tsp bicarbonate of soda*
> *pinch salt.*

Preheat the oven to 180C/Gas 5 and lightly grease a small loaf tin. In the food processor buzz the bananas, sugar, butter, vanilla and salt together till there are no lumps of banana left.

It may curdle, do not worry. Put the flour, bicarbonate and salt in a mixing bowl, you can sift it if you like, I never have. Pour the liquid banana over the flour and mix together. Pour and scrape into loaf tin, making sure it gets right into the corners; bang the base of the tin once on the counter to flatten the top a bit and then bake for about 30–35 minutes until a skewer comes out clean. (You may have to keep an eye on it at the end; the ripe bananas mean there's quite a high sugar content so the top can sometimes catch before the inside is done, particularly if you have a fan oven.) Turn out of the tin and cool on a wire rack. Serve cold in slices, buttered if you like. Keeps brilliantly wrapped in foil and frozen. Also good toasted for breakfast (if it lasts that long).

My Mum's Whisky Cake

175g/6oz sultanas
300ml/½ pint water[1]
4oz/125g butter
150g/5oz caster sugar
1 large egg
175g/6oz plain flour
1 tsp bicarbonate of soda
½ tsp grated nutmeg
½ tsp salt
2 tbsps whisky
1 tbsp lemon juice
75g/2½ oz chopped walnuts.

Preheat oven to 180C/Gas 4. Grease and line two sponge tins. Put the sultanas in a pan with the water (see note) and simmer for 15 minutes. Drain, saving the liquid, and set aside to cool. Cream the butter and sugar together in a food processor (don't worry if you don't have one, you can perfectly well do this by hand, it just takes longer, that's all) until pale and fluffy, then beat in the egg. Fold in the flour, bicarbonate of soda, nutmeg and salt with about two tablespoons of the sultana liquid. Stir in the sultanas, whisky, lemon juice and

---

[1] Now, here you can be crafty. I tend to replace some or all of the water in this recipe with whisky, to make very boozy sultanas indeed. In which case don't boil them, but just soak them overnight so they plump up beautifully.

chopped walnuts. Divide between the sponge tins and bake for about 30 minutes till a skewer comes out clean. Cool on a rack and when cool, ice with:

> *60g/2oz butter*
> *200g/7oz icing sugar*
> *2 tbsps lemon juice*
> *1 dessertsp whisky*
> *walnut halves.*

Buzz together the butter, icing sugar, whisky and lemon juice in a food processor. If the butter is unsalted, you should add a pinch of salt too. You can add a bit more whisky too, if you feel like it. Sandwich the cakes together using half the icing and spread the rest on top. Decorate with walnut halves. Interesting tip, incidentally – decoration always looks better if there's an odd number (i.e. use seven walnut halves round the edge not eight – somehow eight looks twee). This cake can be frozen like this to no ill effect.

Easy Apple Cake

This was very handy the time that Simon came home with three huge baskets full of windfall apples. Read the recipe all the way through before you start, it comes in three sections (like the cake).

> *125g/4oz self raising flour*
> *60g/2oz soft brown sugar*
> *pinch salt*
> *90g/3oz butter*
> *60g/2oz ground almonds*
> *½ beaten egg*
> *½ tsp lemon juice.*

Butter and base line a deep cake tin (round or square). Rub together in a mixing bowl the flour, sugar, salt, butter and 30g/1oz almonds. Bind with the egg and lemon juice. Spread into the tin and sprinkle with the remaining almonds.

> *500g/1lb peeled and sliced eating apples (Cox's are particularly nice)*
> *60g/2oz soft brown sugar.*

Pack the apples evenly over the almond mixture and sprinkle with sugar.

> *60g/2oz self raising flour*
> *150g/5oz soft brown sugar*
> *1 level tsp cinnamon*
> *60g/2oz butter.*

Mix together and blob over the apples (you don't have to be too perfectionist about this, it will spread out as it cooks). Bake for about an hour in a moderate (170–180C/Gas 3–4) oven. Best warm with cream.

Jane's Chocolate Brownies To Die For

These are delicious, and lethal. They are rich, sickly, full of butter and about a squintillion calories a speck. Taste them once and you will never make another brownie recipe in your life. My friend Jane gave me the recipe, so if it is lifted wholesale from someone else's book then my apologies.

> *250g/8oz unsalted butter*
> *125g/4oz cocoa*
> *250g/8oz sugar*
> *pinch salt*
> *4 eggs*
> *tsp vanilla essence*
> *60g/2oz plain flour*
> *90g/3oz chopped roasted hazelnuts (optional)*
> *100g/4oz chopped good quality white chocolate (or more, up to 200g/7oz)*
> *200g/7oz chopped good quality dark chocolate (70% cocoa solids minimum – this is because ordinary dark chocolate is just too sweet and doesn't provide enough flavour contrast. I think. You can use it if you like.)*

Base line and oil a swiss roll tin or baking tray. Heat oven to 190C/Gas 5. Put the butter, cocoa, sugar and salt into a large bowl and melt together, either over a bowl of boiling water or in the microwave. When smoothly mixed, allow to cool for 2 minutes then beat in the eggs and vanilla. Add the flour and mix. Shoot in the nuts if required and the chocolate, and pour into the tray. Bake until just set. (Now, a word of warning. I discovered when I test cooked these for Lucy's birthday recently, that the top feels set after only 10 minutes. The inside is a different story. So I am sorry, Boris, for feeding you raw brownies. Hope you get better soon.) I would say they need to cook for a good 20 minutes. Let cool in the tin for half an hour, then mark into squares, prise out and cool on a rack. These freeze very well (if there are any left, ever).

The Drink

Jasmine, China, Indian, Darjeeling, Earl Grey, Green. Milk or lemon tea are the most popular. Cups and saucers are obviously the way to serve it. However, keep pots warm and in close proximity and thus avoid stewing the tea over a prolonged period.

Invitations

The 'at Home' cards are too formal, so just ring people up. There is no need to give lots of notice unless you serve particularly good food which people will wish to plan their holidays around.

Chapter 4

Supper

I will confess to you now that I have never given a formal dinner party in my life. Even for big parties such as New Year, I reckon that if I've invited people to my house, no matter whether they're wearing ankle length taffeta and a tiara or regardless of how many ancestral silver épergnes are on the table, they're still my friends, and will have to put up with a certain amount of the hostess scuttling into the kitchen halfway through the first course to check on the tomato tart. Society is moving towards a more relaxed style of entertaining anyway. It's just not practical to give grand dinners these days, when everyone is working and time is at a premium. Anyway, with formal dinners in the home there is the danger that the host and hostess get so caught up with protocol and having matching red and white wine glasses and agonising over whether they should have had a calligrapher write the placecards, that they communicate their anxiety to their guests and everyone ends up having a bad time. Far nicer to have fewer people to a more informal supper, in the kitchen, where you can be stirring the Thai fish curry, snorkeling back Sauvignon Blanc, checking the warm chocolate tart, listening to the latest outrage perpetrated by your ex-flatmate's ex-girlfriend, keeping an ear out for the doorbell, moving the soda bread down in the oven, all at once. I hardly ever do a first course for suppers. This is because most people are coming from work and will be late, and if you sit down to three courses at 9.30 p.m., that's an awful lot of food to get through by 11 o'clock. I do often put out a plate of these dead easy palmiers, so people who arrive at 8.30 p.m. don't have to drink for an hour on an empty stomach, which would be unfair. Alternatively, you could serve a packet of bread sticks or a pot of good olive oil and some dukkah, which keeps forever in a jar if you don't use it all at once.

Palmiers
Packet of ready rolled puff pastry, unrolled. Spread with a little Dijon mustard and sprinkle the mustard with grated cheese (Cheddar or Parmesan). Draw a line down the middle (mentally) and on one half put two layers of Parma ham, and on the other, a few lines of anchovies. Roll the two edges up to the centre to form the classic palmier heart shape, and refrigerate for half an hour. Slice thinly, lay on a baking sheet, brush with egg and bake at 190C/Gas 5 for about 10–15 minutes until golden brown and yummy. You can of course do other fillings – chopped black olives, or chopped sun-dried tomatoes, or a thin layer of goats cheese, for example.

Dukkah
Dukkah is a delicious and infinitely flexible North African mixture of toasted nuts and spices. You can add more or less of a thing, depending on how much you like it, or leave it out altogether. You can use hazelnuts instead of almonds, or add chilli flakes, or dried ginger – entirely up to you. Half the fun is experimenting. It's very good, incidentally, on picnics, with cold hard-boiled eggs and sticks of celery.

> *30g/1oz shelled almonds*
> *2 tbsps sesame seeds*
> *1 tsp black mustard seeds*
> *2 tbsps cumin seeds*
> *1 tsp coriander seeds*
> *1 tsp ground cinnamon*
> *1 tsp black peppercorns crushed*
> *½ tsp salt.*

Heat a small heavy frying pan and dry fry the almonds until golden brown. Set aside to cool, then chop roughly. Toast the sesame seeds and put them in a bowl. Repeat with the mustard, cumin and coriander seeds. Either whiz the spices in a (clean) coffee grinder, or grind them with a pestle and mortar. Crush the nuts too to a similar size, and then mix all together with the cinnamon, salt and pepper.

When

Supper can be more easily accommodated within a mid-week scenario as there are fewer courses, less dressing up and less tidying up too. If you are cooking and serving hot food though, you still need people to be there on time, so it would be foolish to ask guests to call round at any time.

Reduced levels of formality allow you to be less anxious about getting the numbers and mix of guests right. Expectations will be different, and impromptu or last minute arranged evenings may sometimes be the most entertaining.

Food

You will probably be happier serving fewer courses or certainly something less filling than a dinner. At supper, it is fine to use a few extra short cuts, as time is limited. You may be able to dispense with cheese and biscuits, and vegetarians could be catered for by adding/subtracting a key ingredient in the main course.

Late Leaving Guests

It is unlikely that everyone will stay too late. If some people are looking a bit too comfortable, you can always suggest 'last orders at the pub before bedtime, busy day tomorrow'. If this does not work or the pubs are closed or are too far away, then rely on sofa beds or the use of taxis.

Cleaning Up

It may still be wise to clear up the last vestige of wine and soak the stains before you retire to bed. Arriving from work to find a cold and crusty fondue, which has been standing for the past 24 hours, can be a little upsetting. Better to take a few weary minutes out, slice up the hardened remains, and place them in the refrigerator. The following evening you may want to add them to bread, requisition a sardine and toast it to save cooking again the next night.

Supper

Suggested Menu
Thai Fish Curry
Lemon Surprise Pudding with Blackcurrants

Domestic entertaining is starting later nowadays and as formality is decreasing, the distinction between supper and dinner parties is becoming increasingly blurred. The number of candles and stains you allow separates a supper from a dinner.

If you invite more people than you have chairs for, accompanied with even fewer glasses, dowdier clothes and easier food then it is supper. So forget the place cards, door attendants and decanters and break out the easy to prepare food.

Thai Fish Curry

> 350g/¾ lb cod fillet, in cubes
> 350g/¾ lb salmon fillet, in cubes
> 250g/½ lb tiger prawns, shell on (raw if possible but cooked if not)
> 2 tbsps flavourless oil
> 1 large red onion, finely sliced
> 1 garlic clove, finely chopped
> 2cm/1in chunk fresh ginger, grated
> 3 stalks lemongrass, finely chopped
> 1 red chilli, chopped
> 1 green chilli, chopped
> 1 tsp ground turmeric
> grated rind and zest of 1 lime
> 300ml/½ pint coconut milk
> 2 tbsps nam pla (fish sauce) or light soy sauce
> 500g/1lb fine green beans
> small bunch fresh coriander, chopped
> small bunch spring onions, chopped.

Fry the onion in the oil until soft and translucent but not browned, and then add the garlic, ginger, lemon grass, chillis and turmeric. Stir around a bit – it will smell delicious. Add the lime rind and juice, coconut milk and nam pla and bring to the boil. If you are doing it in advance, check for seasoning – you may need more lime or chilli – cover, and set aside. You can cook the beans now too – just steam them until lightly cooked, and set aside. When you are ready to finish this off, get the liquid hot again and drop in the fish (add the prawns at this stage if they are raw). Bring back up to the boil and poach the fish until it starts to look a little opaque. Add the cooked prawns now and the cooked beans, to heat through. When the fish is done, stir in the coriander and spring onion, check for seasoning and serve with rice, noodles, or even naan bread.

Lemon Surprise Pudding with Blackcurrants

350g/¾ lb blackcurrants
175g/6oz caster sugar
90g/3oz butter, at room temperature
zest and juice of 4 lemons
4 large eggs, separated
60g/2oz plain flour
pinch salt
170ml/6floz milk

Butter an ovenproof baking dish and preheat the oven to 180C/Gas 4. Put the blackcurrants in the bottom of the dish and sprinkle with 30g/1oz of the sugar. Cream the remaining sugar with the butter till pale and fluffy. Beat in the rind and juice, then beat in the egg yolks one at a time. It may well curdle – don't worry. Beat in the flour and salt, then the milk. In a separate bowl, beat the egg whites to the firm peak stage and fold in (see instructions for cheese soufflé, p. 127, for how to do this). Blob over the currants, then put the dish in a roasting tin and pour in hot water to come halfway up the side of the pudding dish. Bake for about 45 minutes – you will have a lovely light sponge on top and a sharp lemony sauce full of hot explosions of blackcurrants underneath – and serve hot with cold thick cream.

Chapter 5

Dinner Parties

It is impossible to generalise satisfactorily about dinner parties, but a reasonable definition might be 'a group of people, round a table, eating'. Well, yes, but so is supper. 'A dinner party is a group of people, round a table, dressed up, eating'. Yes, but not always. 'A dinner party is a group of people, round a table, probably candlelit, dressed up, eating at least three courses and probably four, and they are not all enjoying themselves as much as they would be if they had been asked for supper, and probably at least one of them would rather be a million miles away, and it's usually the host'. That, unfortunately, is more like it.

Why are dinner parties so stressful? Do not believe magazines which say that they are easy and stress-free. They are not. Supper is a breeze. Pull the shepherd's pie out of the oven, plonk it on the kitchen table and away you go. Dinner, on the other hand, implies so much more. More elaborate food, more courses, more wineglasses, more dressing up, more silverware, flower arrangements, the wedding china, drinks beforehand and port after – by the time you go to bed you will have used every pan, plate, napkin and glass in the house and you will be exhausted. My advice is, if you possibly can, have supper instead.

But sometimes, you just have to do dinner. The Duty Dinner, the Having The Boss Round Dinner, the 60th Birthday Dinner, the Pre-Hunt-Ball Dinner, the Showing Off My Famous Friend To My Less Famous Friends Dinner – all valid categories, all unavoidable. Grit your teeth and do it, and try if you possibly can to enjoy it. Just accept that it is rare that one truly enjoys one's own party, but who knows? Maybe it'll turn out to be more enjoyable than you expect.

One of the main reasons that dinner is so stressful is the sheer number of factors to take into account. Are you having a duty dinner party, or a celebratory evening, or have you got some London friends down for the weekend? Is your table small and round, or an ancestral skating rink of 19th century French fruitwood? Is Lucy allergic to dairy products? Is Lord Snoggit the sort to take offence if he is not seated to the right of the hostess? Do you have enough red wine? Will the Aga faint and die halfway through baking the chocolate and ginger soufflé? Have you got too many people? Or too few? Interestingly this is probably the one area where you could point out the difference between supper and dinner. Supper implies small, intimate – to my mind, no more than six or maximum seven of you sitting – whereas 'dinner' with its greater formality and ceremony tends to mean eight people or more. Six people can have one single conversation where everyone is contributing; eight tend to split up into threes and twos. It's a question of balance.

And that is the great worry about dinner parties – getting the balance right. Whether it's balance of menu, balance of numbers, balance of friends, balance of political views, whatever. There are vast quantities of books written about how to get it right, so none of this is going to be news to anyone. Unlike the rest of the recipes in this book, there is no recipe for having a 100% guaranteed successful dinner party. The obvious rules of thumb are:

- Don't invite people if you know they actively dislike one another or are having a clandestine affair with the other half of one of the couples present
- Don't, unless you really enjoy fistfights in the sitting room, invite people with rabidly held and opposing political views (and for that matter, unless you're prepared to sit through an evening's soapboxing, don't invite too many people of the same political viewpoint either)
- Don't invite a new friend to a dinner party where everyone else round the table has known each other since childhood.

With the exception of the Duty Dinner, the people round your dining table are your friends and you are inviting them because you want them to enjoy themselves – it's not a purely selfish exercise. Duty Dinners are different. These are for people you would normally only invite to your house if a knife is held to your throat, and what's worse, you have to inflict this couple on people whom you consider your friends. It could

Dinner Parties

be the irritating neighbours who were so good that time that your roof blew off when you were on holiday in Tuscany, or your old school friend with the completely unsuitable second wife, or your other half's boss. The question then is, do you (a) dilute them, by inviting at least eight other people, thus risking all your friends referring to 'that grim dinner party where John and Anthea had that terrible couple'; or do you (b) only expose them to one or two really good friends, who would do the same for you in your position? This is a terrible dilemma and one that only you can answer.

Whichever you do, to ease the burden on yourself, in what will quickly become the rallying theme of this entire book, for dinner parties you must do as much in advance as possible. I come from a family where my mother cooks solidly for weeks on end beforehand if she knows she has a spate of people coming to stay (we're talking about a woman with two full size fridge freezers and a chest freezer, in a two bedroom flat), and not only that, but she has been known to set the table for Christmas lunch three days in advance and cover it with newspapers to keep the dust off. So plan, clean, tidy up, move the furniture around – ahead of time.

Nine times out of ten, you won't have a nice long leisurely day to prepare this food. You will get home from work late (it's invariably on days that you know you want to get away on time that a crisis blows up at 5.30 p.m.) and will have to set the table, move the drying laundry, hide the more embarrassing CDs, tidy the *Hellos* off the coffee table, etc., before your guests arrive. While there is something to be said for spur of the moment cookery (of which more below), if you know you are having eight people for dinner on Thursday night, here is the rule: Malice Aforethought. Unless you want to spend the precious hour you have between getting home from work and the first guest arriving in the kitchen getting hot and cross and worried that your pommes dauphinoises are running behind schedule, then the only thing to do is get as much of the cooking as you can done ahead of time. I cannot stress this enough. Get it out of the way so you can actually talk to your guests when you see them and don't wind up having a heart attack through stress.

You need to set aside an evening earlier in the week to get the shopping and then the cooking done. If possible, do it the night immediately preceding your dinner party, so the vegetables are fresh and you can keep the casserole in the fridge overnight rather than having to freeze it and worry about it defrosting in time. I'm sorry, but sacrificing one evening ahead of time will save your blood pressure and quite possibly your relationship with your other half.

So you need to be aware ahead of time what you are going to cook. Sorry to state the blindingly obvious. You need to have thought ahead, planned what you are going to make, and made a shopping list. It is all very well reading smug dictats from professional chefs which tell us never to go shopping with fixed ideas, but rather to rely on what is good in the market that morning. However lovely this idea might be, in practice it is simply not feasible. Bear in mind two things. They are professionals, and can make up recipes and balance menus in their heads as they go along. So if they spot a really spectacular looking turbot, they can jettison the venison they had planned on and rejig the entire meal accordingly. The mere thought of doing this in my head would send me into a flat spin. 'But now that I'm doing turbot I can't do smoked salmon to start and the pudding is too creamy and bland to go after fish, oh help, maybe I can do chocolate tart, oh but how much icing sugar goes into the pastry and do I have enough eggs' etc., and eventually I have to be helped to the nearest seat. Anyway, most of us don't even have a market nearby – we're relying on the supermarket, and the great thing about supermarkets is that it is in their interest to have a wide range of good quality and more importantly *available* ingredients. You can be sure that if you've planned to make boeuf en daube followed by plum tart, you will find all the bits that you need, plus all the vegetables, crisps, fizzy water, extra black peppercorns, whatever, under one roof. And this is a godsend for anyone trying to save time. By all means, if you get to the supermarket and see that the fish counter has got fresh halibut on special, then buy it. What I'm saying is, for heaven's sake don't feel you have to. Don't ever feel guilty about not taking the 'fly by the seat of your pants' approach to cooking for a dinner party. Certainly, you can be a bit more relaxed if it's just the two of you (see the chapter later on Impromptu Entertaining), or if you're cooking for your family, but if you're having an organised Dinner Party, capital D capital P, then a bit of thinking ahead of time is absolutely necessary, unless you want to be hysterical in the kitchen making sauce maltaise for the broccoli 20 minutes before the guests arrive.

And don't forget, shopping can be more time consuming than the actual act of putting the meal together, so allow yourself plenty of time to do your shopping, whether you do it all in the supermarket or you go all round the houses to the organic greengrocer, the deli, the cheese shop, the butcher, baker and candlestick maker.

The Theory

It is important to be organised. If people have taken the trouble to visit you, it is polite to be in the same room as your guests and not to find distraction in a failing Bearnaise sauce in a distant kitchen. Technical problems are no excuse for non-participation in the evening's social events. Remember that even after a short while your guests will become embarrassed and even agitated.

Attempt to strike a balance between preparing some good food and socialising with your guests. If you have hired help or a partner, then they can perform either of these roles with you. The relative merits of your cooking and your conversational skills should determine who does what, the raconteur will hold court whilst the other shells the peas.

The Basics

If you are the owner of a large dining room, with enough room for people to walk round the outside, then all the better. If the living room doubles as a kitchen diner then some thought has to be given as to how many people you can accommodate and whether shoe horning extra trestle tables in from the garage is really appropriate.

An extendible table that can seat four comfortably, and six normally, is often highly useful. The fun arises from how creatively you use the four matching chairs. You may need to beg, borrow and steal extra chairs. If you can keep a few folding chairs in a spare room then your entertaining options are increased. Folding chairs can be comfortable especially if you co-ordinate them with cushion tie backs in keeping with the room's décor.

The actual number of seats available is not a totally limiting factor. You can cook for 20 by sitting everybody on cushions on the floor. However, this is not a suggested format for your boss or elderly relatives.

Consider the size of the table. If you plan to cook six courses, involving soups, sorbets, fish, casseroles, vegetables, profiteroles, cheese, all accompanied with wine, then check the table capacity and bear in mind that you will need to wash the plates mid-course. You can employ the custom of certain countries on 'the continent' by asking guests to retain their plates to avoid having to do this.

Remember that many local supermarket chains hire out catering equipment such as glassware which in many cases you can return unwashed. You should check with grocers, hire companies and off-licences as to what equipment and supplies they can deliver.

If the table is in the kitchen, then consider how appropriate it is to cook in the same room as you will eat in. A guest who sees you dropping the roast lamb on the floor and swearing at the cracked china can feel uncomfortable. The amount of available space and your living environment will determine the amount of preparation needed before your guests arrive.

Guest Lists

Getting the right people together is part of the art of planning a really good dinner party. The issues to consider are the compatibility of the guests, and the benefit of mixing the pack with a few wild cards to add something a little different. Having the same people regularly over to dinner can become boring and lack stimulation.

At the other extreme though, combining all the people you have had invitations from but could not bear to accept, as well as that boring couple you met on holiday who actually took you up on your offer of dinner when you get back, is a high risk strategy.

Preparation

It is essential to do what you can the night *before* your guests arrive. There are tactical benefits to this as we are all hopeless optimists in the kitchen. Guests invited for 7p.m. cannot be kept waiting till 1a.m. A 35 minute pasta dish that goes astray can find your guests becoming satiated with tortilla chips long before the meal. Your chilli may be excellent but if it does not arrive at the table until the available alcohol is drunk, the party could go horribly wrong. Elaborate compliments on the quality of your cooking may seem hollow from guests whom 30 minutes later are asleep or dancing to *Agadoo*.

How to Invite

Communication is important in all aspects of life and none more so than on the invitation. There is important information to impart and one or two matters that they must tell you. In theory, it all seems simple. In theory yes.

The invitation, whether verbal or written must contain most (if not all) of the following:

- Where – A house number, street and map if needed – your name at the very least
- When – Date and time. The considerate guest invited at 7 for 7.30p.m. would arrive at 7.15p.m.
- Why – Is a special event being celebrated?
- What to wear
- What to bring
- How to reply.

In a perfect scenario, guests will never arrive before, and not too much after, their invited time. Consider how tardy certain guests customarily are. If they are likely to arrive an hour late, then tell them to arrive an hour early. This 'game' can only be played a few times. The indication of a special occasion intimates whether guests should think about buying you a present. This of course saves them the embarrassment of turning up without a gift when your other friends have presented theirs. A dress code is somewhat obvious for fancy dress affairs but it may be especially important to tell the long-haired hippy that everyone else is wearing a suit. Your guests may bring games for a themed evening, and perhaps on a low cost evening they may each bring a different course. As you would not want to end up with six potato salads – try to co-ordinate their contributions beforehand. If you really do not want them to bring a bottle then you should tell them something along the lines of "Don't bring anything other than a sparkling personality and a will to eat." Flowers to say thank you afterwards is a great touch. Above all ask them to call or write to confirm their attendance because the food shopping is paramount. The correct way of presenting your invitation is dealt with in more detail in *Debrett's Guide to Correspondence*.

The Implication of Your Invitation

The style of the invitation you use is indicative of the level of formality required for your dinner. An embossed formal invitation suggests smart dress. The back of an envelope or a cigarette packet indicates something quite different.

'At Home' cards may be used with the words 'Dinner 8 for 8.30 p.m.', written by hand. The high street printers are able to personalise them with your address.

If appropriate, guidelines concerning dress must be given by you. However, allow for a liberal interpretation of words such as 'casual' or 'smart casual'.

Posting a written invitation allows your potential guests the opportunity to consult with their diaries without being placed on the spot. Moreover, it does not allow the potential guest to quiz you on important matters, such as who else is coming. A sign of good taste and friendship is allowing your friends the opportunity to excuse themselves for non-attendance in their own time. It is often best to write, as this conveys a sense of occasion and then by all means follow up with a telephone call if they have not already replied.

Technology

A more modern and informal approach might be to use the technology of a fax or e-mail if you think your friends would be likely to read them. Some e-mail programs have a facility whereby a recipient responds by voting yes or no. You must also remember that faxes are often not private. These methods may be quick but it would seem more appropriate for the last minute arrangement.

Other Considerations

It is important to find out if there are any food issues such as allergies, vegetarianism, diabetes, and so on. Your guests should volunteer this information, but it is worthwhile to ask them in any case. In order to avoid sending out a dietary questionnaire, why not put a small written note on the back of the invitation, or make a quick call to elicit the information? Your guests will appreciate your care and thought. The key to getting the right people to attend is to give them enough notice and issue a few key reminders to the more forgetful of your guests. Notice periods depend upon whom you are inviting and what kind of commitment they need in relation to how busy they are. Mid-week entertaining offers different pressures from the weekend. More people may be available during the week, but it is likely that the partying will be less intense if they have to be up early for work the next day.

If your attendees have children and live miles away, then it might be good form to give them a couple of months' notice and a few options of dates for them to pick from. This leaves the ball in their court as to when a family visit would work best for them.

Replies

Although good manners require your guests to respond to invitations with RSVP on them, they might be late in doing so, or forget altogether. In this case, chase up with a telephone call as you will need to know the following:

- Yes, I can attend and am looking forward to it
- No I cannot attend – with appropriate excuse, or reason for non attendance
- Yes, but I am vegetarian/allergic to nuts etc. – (See *Catering for Fussy Eaters* below)
- Yes, but my brother is in town, so will only attend if I can bring him – respond accordingly.

If people say 'Yes' and then do not attend then this is the height of rudeness unless a truly dreadful calamity has occurred.

Suggested Menu

Glazed Garlic Mushroom and Asparagus Crêpes
Roast Monkfish with Bacon and a Red Pepper Sauce
Roasted Green Beans
Orange Frangipane Pudding with Poached Orange Slices

This has a rich and delicious starter followed by a lighter fish dish, and then a pudding which started off life as a tart, but in the interests of health, I decided you could perfectly well have it without the pastry. Please feel free to reinstate the pastry case if you like. Frangipane is just a posh culinary term for a mixture of almonds, butter, sugar and egg. I quite often make a chocolate version and serve it with poached pears.

The green beans are my most favourite vegetable in the world ever. You won't believe that you could like a vegetable so much. I make them all the time and end up eating them and ignoring everything else on my plate. I don't serve potatoes with the fish, as I think there's probably been enough carbohydrate in the crêpes already. But if you feel the lack then I would suggest plain boiled baby new potatoes, or if you were doing the fish without the crêpes to start then little cubes sautéd till crunchy and golden with rosemary and garlic would be heaven.

Glazed Garlic Mushroom and Asparagus Crêpes

The great thing about this recipe is that you can cook the crêpes weeks ahead of time (up to three months ahead of time, for heaven's sake, although if you have planned a menu that far in advance then I think you should seek help) and freeze them, interleaved with greaseproof paper, for bringing out and assembling on the day. Or, of course, you can avoid having to make crêpes at all by using an English muffin (the sort you use for Eggs Benedict), although this does make it quite a solid dish, the English muffin not being exactly renowned for its light and fluffy qualities.

First make your crêpes. If you have your own favourite savoury crêpe recipe, then use it. Otherwise, here is a pretty good all-purpose one:

> *125g/4oz plain flour*
> *300ml/½ pint milk*
> *1 egg*
> *1 egg yolk*
> *2 tbsps melted butter*
> *salt and pepper*
> *a little extra melted butter for cooking.*

Now then. There are two schools of thought for pancake batter. One says, make a well in the centre of the sifted flour and seasoning, break the egg (and egg yolk) into it, and gradually beat in the milk and melted butter until a thick, smooth batter is formed. The other way (my way) says, put everything *except* the flour into a food processor, whiz it together, then turn the motor to slow and add the flour gradually but steadily. Transfer to a jug. Either way, if the mixture can sit for an hour or so before use, so much the better. (If you're using this recipe for other fillings, don't forget you can always add interesting flavours to the batter – chopped fresh herbs, or a tablespoon or so of grated Parmesan, or lemon rind for fish.) Heat a small frying pan, brush it with melted butter, and pour in just enough batter to cover the pan. Cook until the underside is golden, then turn the pancake by tossing it (yeah right) or using a palette knife or fish slice to help it over. I will tell you now, the first pancake is always, always, a mutant. Set it aside, feed it to the dog, eat it yourself – but it will not be socially acceptable. This is one of those inexplicable facts, up there with where do all the biros go and why London Transport time (three minutes till the next tube train) bears no resemblance to actual earth time. Continue to make pancakes, brushing the pan with melted butter as and when necessary, till you have no batter left. This will make about 12, which is more than you need, but don't worry, they are nice pancakes and you will find you will use them. I confess I tend to eat them standing up by the cooker. Quality control, you see, it's important. Interleave them with greaseproof paper and freeze till needed.

Then, per pancake, you will need:

> *2–3 spears cooked asparagus (depending on how fat and juicy your asparagus is, and how much you like your friends)*

> about 2 heaped tbsps cooked mushrooms – method given below
> some hollandaise – the quantity given below is on the generous side for this recipe but it's hard to make less.

For the mushrooms:

> 500g/1lb fresh mushrooms (wild are good, but I would use a mixture of wild and cultivated as all wild would be too rich), roughly chopped
> 30g/1oz butter
> 2 cloves garlic, crushed
> 2–3 tbsps hollandaise from the quantity you have made.

Fry the mushrooms in the butter, slowly at first until the juices start to be released, then turn up the heat to drive off the excess water (and mushrooms do produce a lot of liquid). This will probably take about 10 minutes in total. Stir in the crushed garlic and the hollandaise (you don't really want to 'see' the hollandaise, it is just there to bind the mushrooms together slightly). Check for seasoning and set aside till required.

For the hollandaise:

There is no mystery to hollandaise. It is just a question of confidence. If it curdles, it curdles. Start again. It's only eggs and butter – hardly difficult to get hold of. If you are really truly incapable of making hollandaise, then please don't buy the stuff in jars, it is foul and tastes of udder ointment.

Classic hollandaise is made with a reduction of tarragon vinegar and water. Now call me pedantic, and I'm sorry, Escoffier, I must have missed the point, but why add water to vinegar in order to then reduce it? Hello? Reducing is just driving off water, surely? Why add it in the first place?

> 2 egg yolks
> 225g/8oz butter, melted
> juice of half a lemon (or more), or 1–2 tbsps tarragon vinegar
> salt and pepper.

Dinner Parties

Once again, two schools of thought on the hollandaise front. One is very cool, and is made in the blender. It says, buzz the egg yolks and lemon juice or vinegar till thick and fluffy, then with the motor still running add the hot melted butter, slowly at first then more quickly, until the sauce has the consistency of mayonnaise. Check for seasoning. Now, I have never succeeded with this. I prefer to make mine the old fashioned way, which means getting the egg yolks and lemon juice into a bowl over a pan of barely simmering water (please don't go buying any expensive bains marie, will you? If you have a basket steamer this is all you need) and whisking till fluffy. Then, add the melted butter, a teaspoon at a time at first, beating in well between each addition. Once you've incorporated about half of the butter, you can add more at a time. Careful the bowl doesn't get too hot or the sauce will split. You can, if you do have a curdling disaster, start again by taking another egg yolk and beating the curdled mixture into it. But I have confidence in you and your sauce will be fine first time. You see? You can keep hollandaise warm for a bit over the barely simmering water but I warn you, it will split if it gets too warm. It's almost better (assuming your kitchen is not utterly freezing) to leave it to one side off the heat, not in a draught, somewhere at, say, warm room temperature – if it thickens up a bit that's fine, because as you'll see you're going to put it under a grill anyway.

While we're talking about hollandaise, if you make it with orange juice not lemon juice (and if you can get blood orange juice then please make this at least once in your life as the colour is just amazing), and possibly put a bit of orange rind in the sauce, and yes it might need a drop or two of lemon juice depending on how sweet the orange was, then you will have made sauce maltaise which is knockout with broccoli and cod which has been rolled in a mixture of quick-cook polenta grains, Cajun seasoning, chilli pepper flakes and dried oregano and then baked in the oven with a drizzle of oil.

To assemble the crêpes, put a couple of asparagus spears on each crêpe, top with a couple of tablespoons of mushrooms and roll up from one side. Repeat with the remaining pancakes (or as many as you have mushroom mixture for), put them in a lightly buttered baking dish or on individual ovenproof plates, and warm through gently in the oven for 10 or so minutes. Spoon a generous streak of hollandaise down the back of each crêpe and flash under a hot grill till the hollandaise is just catching. Serve at once.

Roast Monkfish with Bacon and a Red Pepper Sauce

You will already have the oven on for warming through the crêpes, so if you have this all ready to go, then all you'll have to do is turn up the heat in the oven, warm through the sauce and put the fish and beans in the oven.

> *4–6 small monkfish tails (about 700g/1½ lbs), membranes removed*
> *8–12 rashers streaky bacon (you will be wrapping it round the fish, so use your judgement). You could also use Parma ham*
> *2–3 cloves garlic, cut into slivers*
> *one or two branches fresh thyme or rosemary*
> *olive oil*
> *170ml/6floz fish or chicken stock, or dry white wine, or water (or any combination thereof).*

Stab the fish with a little sharp knife (I use Naughty Knife) and insert slivers of garlic. Wrap the bacon round and secure with a toothpick. Heat a couple of tablespoons of olive oil and quickly sear the fish on all sides. Transfer to a roasting tin, tuck in the herb sprigs, and pour over the liquid. Set aside till needed.

Make the red pepper sauce. This looks complicated – don't worry, it's not, it's just a long list of ingredients. The celery, onion, carrot and garlic are the Italian *battuta* – a flavouring method whereby the vegetables aren't integral to the sauce, they just give up their flavour and add a lovely savoury base note.

> *1 large onion, chopped*
> *2 sticks celery, chopped*
> *1 large carrot, chopped*
> *1 clove garlic, crushed*
> *1 small sprig thyme or rosemary (whichever you have used above)*
> *2 tbsps olive oil*
> *60g/2oz unsalted butter*
> *500g/1lb red peppers, seeded and chopped*

Dinner Parties

> 125g/4oz tomatoes, chopped
> 150ml/5floz dry white wine
> 300ml/10floz chicken or fish stock
> 1 tbsp tomato purée
> 1 tsp red wine vinegar
> ½ tsp caster sugar
> fresh basil or tarragon.

Fry the onion, celery, carrot, garlic and herb in the oil and butter for a few minutes till softened. Add the peppers and tomatoes and cook for a few minutes, then add the stock, wine, purée, vinegar and sugar. Bring to the boil, cover and simmer for 20–25 minutes till fairly thick. Liquidise and check for consistency and seasoning. If you want a perfectly smooth sauce, pass it through a sieve (I prefer it a bit nubbly). Set aside till needed. When you want it, heat through, tear up the basil or tarragon and stir in just before serving.

To finish the fish, put the oven on to very high (230C/Gas 8) and roast for 20–30 minutes, turning once or twice. Remove the tails to a platter and keep them warm. Pour the pan juices into the red pepper sauce, add the torn fresh basil or tarragon and check again for seasoning and consistency. Using a sharp knife, carve the tails into chunky slices. If this were supper, I'd let the guests do their own knifework. This is kinder though, and more elegant. Fan out the slices on each plate and pour a streak of sauce down the slices. Serve with the beans. This is also nice, if you have the inclination, with a warm salad of plum tomato slices. Simply skin about 1–1½ nice firm plum tomatoes per head (depending on size) by dropping them in boiling water and then slipping off the skins. Slice them fairly thickly across the equator, and warm them through very briefly in a little olive oil and lemon juice, not so much that they start to cook, but literally just to warm them. Sprinkle with chopped chives or basil.

Roasted Green Beans

> Enough green beans per person (I would allow about 600g/1¼ lb for four polite people, but more might be good)
> 2 tbsps flavourless oil.

Top and tail the beans, wash and dry them, then toss them in the oil. Spread evenly on a baking tray and roast for 10–15 minutes on a shelf underneath the fish (so they'll need to go in about 10–15 minutes after you put the fish in). Keep an eye on them and when they are crisp and shiny and patched with brown they are ready. For once, these are nicer over rather than underdone. If they are still limp then cook them longer. You want them verging on brittle. I am warning you – they go cold in about 2 seconds, and nothing you do will keep them warm. It doesn't matter, people devour them irrespective of temperature.

Orange Frangipane Pudding with Poached Orange Slices

2 eggs
100g/3½ oz caster sugar
grated zest and juice 1 orange
2 tsps lemon juice
2 tsps Cointreau/Grand Marnier or other orange flavoured liqueur
90g/3oz unsalted butter, at room temperature
pinch salt
100g/3½ oz ground almonds.

This is nicest made in individual tart tins, but unless you are (a) a professional cook or (b) hopelessly anal, these are very low on most people's list of kitchen priorities, so I tend to make this in a lightly oiled 9in fluted metal tart tin with a removable base.

Whisk the eggs and sugar till pale and fluffy, then add the remaining ingredients and whiz till just combined. Pour into the tart tin and bake at 190C/Gas 5 for about 20–25 minutes until golden brown.

For the topping:
90g/3oz sugar
150ml/5floz water
6–8 cloves (optional)
3–4 thin skinned oranges, thinly sliced
1 tbsp orange marmalade or apricot jam
1 tsp orange liqueur.

In a large pan combine the sugar, water and cloves, bring to the boil and simmer for 5 minutes. Add the orange slices, turn the heat down and simmer gently for 3–5 minutes until the pith goes slightly translucent, but not so far that they start to disintegrate. Fish them out with a slotted spoon and arrange them prettily on top of the frangipane. Put your grill on. Boil away the poaching syrup with the marmalade and liqueur until you have a thick sticky syrup. Pour or brush this over the orange slices (pick off the cloves and any escaped orange pips) and then flash the frangipane under the grill until the edges of the oranges just start to caramelise. Leave to cool. Serve in thin wedges with crème fraîche.

Catering for Fussy Eaters

Dietary requirements, fads, and those grey areas in between may be yet another problem for the harassed chef, and you need to be aware of these in the early stages of planning your meal. There seems to be a rise in the incidence of allergies that can be dangerous and possibly fatal. Wheat, nuts, and dairy products are all capable of triggering allergic reactions, and particular care should be taken with soft cheese if any of your guests are pregnant. Seafood allergies are common too, and it is also worth remembering that many people believe that serving seafood – particularly oysters – with spirits is not a good idea, because the hard liquor will 'seize' the delicate seafood into some kind of weird rubbery mass in one's stomach. Personally, I wouldn't serve seafood with spirits purely because anything as strong as whisky or gin stuns the tastebuds, and you can't taste what you're eating, which seems a terrible waste of prawns. And anyway, how do these people deal with Lobster Thermidor (which is, after all, lobster with cream and cheese and brandy?)

Diabetics

Diabetes sufferers are generally well aware of their needs and are prepared in terms of their condition, but it is essential that food is served regularly to diabetics to prevent long periods without sustenance. An insulin dependant diabetic who injects anticipating a meal can become ill if food is not consumed even 20–30 minutes after an injection. This will vary from person to person and the periods of non-eating can be longer but they could also be shorter. You should check with your diabetic guest carefully.

Vegetarians

Vegetarianism, veganism, and fruitarianism can be associated with a religion but are often more a lifestyle choice. It is important to be specific when using these terms. Many people believe vegetarianism means that it is fine to cook chicken, while there are those who include fish and those who do not. The composition of the meal is your choice, but quite often a first course can easily provide a vegetarian option while being suitable for everyone, while you might need to provide some options for the main course.

Many vegetarian chefs will not cook meat for other people either for physical or moral reasons. In many cases they will attempt to prepare a vegetarian meal that is good enough for most omnivores and which suspends the craving to eat meat, at least for an evening.

Catering for vegetarians can be tricky. It does largely depend on how much notice you have as to what you give them. If they pitch up at your door and only then announce their inability to eat God's creatures, then they deserve a store cupboard supper. Baked beans on toast should do it. If they let you know ahead of time, though, it gives you the chance to find out whether they eat fish, in which case you can give everybody a fish main course and a vegetarian starter. Quite a lot of starters are vegetarian anyway, for example the Roasted Yellow Pepper or Spinach Soups from the Lunch chapter. If they don't eat fish, then if you are a good host you will assemble a meal whose components, taken without the chunk of animal protein, will also be a vegetarian option. Curries are a good idea, since most people have taken on board that saag aloo or dhal generally accompany the lamb rogan josh. Or cook something with mushrooms. Somehow the texture of mushrooms lets you think you're eating meat. But let us not even darken our doorstep with the vegan. Life is too short. Only genuine allergies accepted. Actually to be fair, there are a couple of things you can do for vegans (one of which is show them the door) – and although they are going to be nut and/or pulse based, if you don't actually point this out then you may get away with it with your other guests.

Dinner Parties

Suggested Vegetarian Menu
Courgette 'Snails'
Pasta with Wild Mushroom and Tomato Sauce
Pecan Pie Squares

Courgette 'Snails'

> 6 medium courgettes
> 125ml/4floz olive oil
> 2–3 tbsps freshly chopped flatleaf parsley
> 2–3 tbsps freshly chopped basil
> rind and juice of 1 lemon
> 1 clove garlic, crushed
> plank of feta cheese, in cubes.

Trim the ends off the courgettes and slice lengthways about ½ cm/¼ in thick. Grill, either under normal grill or on a cast-iron ridged grill pan, until tender but not too charred. Mix the olive oil, herbs, lemon and garlic in a shallow non-metallic dish and, as the courgette strips are removed from the grill, drop them into the marinade to cool. When cool, wrap each strip round a chunk of feta and secure with a toothpick (now you know why we have called them 'snails'). Leave in the remaining juices, turning them over from time to time, until ready to serve (overnight is fine, but bring them out of the refrigerator a little ahead of time as the cold stunts the flavours).

Pasta with Wild Mushroom and Tomato Sauce

> 1 onion chopped
> olive oil
> 2 cloves garlic, crushed
> 2 ×400g tins chopped tomatoes
> ½ tsp dried oregano
> 1 chopped fresh red chilli
> 1 tsp red wine vinegar
> 1 tsp sugar
> 1 small packet dried mushrooms (about 40–50g)
> 2 tbsps chopped flatleaf parsley.

Make the usual tomato sauce by slowly frying the onion in about a tablespoon of olive oil till golden and limp. Add the garlic, tomato and oregano, turn up the heat and boil hard with the lid off for about 5 minutes to reduce slightly. Add the chilli, vinegar, sugar and mushrooms and simmer for 20 minutes till thickened. Normally, you would soak the mushrooms in warm water to reconstitute, but in this case as your sauce is fairly liquid, there should be no need, although you should keep an eye on your simmering sauce in case the mushrooms suck up all the liquid. Check for seasoning. Stir in the parsley and serve over tagliatelle (ideally), although any pasta will do.

Pecan Pie Squares

Use packet ready rolled shortcrust pastry. You may need to flatten it out a little more, it doesn't want to be too thick

> *150ml/5floz melted unsalted butter*
> *60ml/2floz maple syrup (if you like it – otherwise you could use honey)*
> *60ml/2floz golden syrup*
> *125g/4oz brown sugar*
> *30ml/1floz double cream*
> *500g/1lb shelled pecans, coarsely chopped.*

Line a baking tray with silicon paper and trim the pastry to fit it. Prick all over and bake at 180C/Gas 4 for about 15 minutes till just going golden. Mix the remaining ingredients, making sure the pecans are thoroughly coated. Spread over the crust and bake for 25–30 minutes more. Cool completely before cutting into squares. Eat with ice cream and hear your tooth enamel scream in horror.

Vegans

Vegan cookery takes a little more imagination, and much more care. A great deal of what people eat could be termed vegan anyway, so it is wrong to assume automatically that you need to prepare dozens of different meals if some of your guests are vegan.

Dinner Parties

Fruitarians

Fruitarians believe the only food that should be eaten is that which dies naturally, that is to say it falls from a tree or plant of its own volition. Fruitarians are extremely difficult to cater for and you should perhaps take advice from the guests themselves if this occasion arises.

Dieters

Dieters can usually scrape off rich sauces, have no sour cream on their baked potato, or eat like normal humans for one meal and then get back on the straight and narrow tomorrow. If you are intent on helping the dieter out, though, and have had some notice, grill something or lightly sear something, and serve any sauce separately. The onion marmalade with Parma ham and asparagus starter which appears in *Cooking to Impress* (see page 139) is ideal, as they can eat the vegetables and lean meat and leave the cheese and rich marmalade alone. If you are feeling truly generous, you could make the dieters a salsa verde, which, although it has real knockout flavours, is not very calorific (and non-dieters seem to like it too). As a general rule, cook plain, boiled or steamed vegetables and have some hollandaise or even extra virgin olive oil available for your other guests. Pudding can be fresh fruit, but you must make it interesting. No-one likes chilly, miserable, sour Granny Smiths. Cherries, pineapple, nectarines, blueberries are wonderful especially if you have extra thick Greek yoghurt and crunchy brown sugar available for non-dieters. Alternatively, you can make a real fruit jelly – passionfruit, or the terribly voguish rhubarb. Sorbets are also good, as although they are high in sugar they are still low in fat, and you can serve masses of cream or even another ice cream alongside to jolly it up.

Suggested Menu for Dieters

Fresh Broad Beans, Peas and Parma Ham
Seared Moroccan Salmon
Roasted Vegetable Couscous
Chocolate Sorbet (with coffee ice cream, maybe)

Fresh Broad Beans, Peas and Parma Ham

This recipe is especially good is if the beans and peas are your own, because you can then be smug about your 'home grown' produce. However, supermarket vegetables are so varied and plentiful now, that they provide a suitable alternative. This recipe is also great for an informal lunch party or kitchen supper.

> *enormous of pile fresh broad bean pods (try to obtain smaller ones if possible, the big ones can be a bit mealy)*
> *a large pile of fresh pea pods*
> *a large plate of thinly sliced Parma ham*
> *loaf of ciabatta*
> *fresh, unsalted butter.*

Put all these items in the centre of the table. Everyone helps themselves and pods their own peas or beans. Even people who claim not to like broad beans will be won over by the freshness of them and the combination of crisp, raw bright green bean with soft, salty ham and a glass of cold white wine is fantastic.

Seared Moroccan Salmon

The North African chermoula marinade has become fashionable lately, and it is delicious and more importantly, easy. If you do not like a particular herb or spice, simply omit it and if you think an alternative would work, then use it instead. This version is slightly less authentic than most, but anise and fennel go well with fish. You could also add a teaspoon of crumbled dried bay leaf if desired.

> *4 175g/6oz salmon steaks or fillets, skinned*
> *1 star anise pod, pounded with a pestle and mortar (or, to be realistic, I more often use a good teaspoon of Chinese five spice powder)*
> *1 tsp fennel seeds, crushed*
> *1 tsp ground turmeric (to be authentic, use ground saffron, but the flavour has a tendency to be lost)*
> *2 tbsps ground cumin*
> *½ tsps ginger (fresh is wonderful but dried is a close second)*
> *½ tsp ground coriander*

Dinner Parties

> $^1\!/_2$ tsp ground cinnamon
> 1 tsp ground black pepper
> $^1\!/_2$ tsp dried red chilli flakes.

Mix the herbs together and coat the salmon with them, marinate for at least an hour. Meanwhile, make the roasted red pepper sauce:

> 4 red peppers, roasted and skinned
> 2 tbsps olive oil
> 1 tbsp sherry vinegar (or you could use cider vinegar)
> 2 tbsps paprika
> 2 tsps ground cumin
> 1 clove garlic
> Tabasco, fresh red chilli, chilli flakes – to taste
> salt and pepper.

Purée all together and add Tabasco or other spice to taste. Check for seasoning. Add a little water to slacken it if it is too thick. Heat a heavy baking tray in the oven to 190C/Gas 5 and when it is hot, place it over one of the elements on the hob of your oven (to keep it hot). Smear a little flavourless oil on it and slam the salmon down onto it, it will sizzle and catch. Turn the salmon over and sear the other side. Then put the salmon in the hot oven and bake for about 8 minutes depending on the thickness of the pieces of fish. (A good rule of thumb is 10 minutes per 2cm/1in of height, and salmon should be under rather than overdone.) Serve with roasted vegetable couscous, some natural yoghurt, and the roasted red pepper sauce.

Roasted Vegetable Couscous
It is difficult to give precise instructions for how to cook couscous, since instructions on the back of the packet do vary according to which brand you are using, but as a rough guide, 250g/8oz couscous should be ample for four, especially as you are adding vegetables to it. But do read the packet in case the amount of water suggested is hugely different.

> 1 courgette, sliced (see p. 130 for diatribe on how to cut up cylindrical vegetables please)

> 1 red pepper, sliced
> 1 yellow pepper, sliced
> 1 red onion, sliced
> 1 clove garlic, crushed
> olive oil
> 250g/8oz couscous
> 300ml/10floz boiling water with a stock cube added
> 2 level tbsps chopped fresh mint.

Toss the prepared vegetables with the garlic and a drizzle of olive oil and roast at 200C/Gas 6 for about 30–40 minutes till tender and just beginning to catch at the edges. Put the couscous in a heatproof bowl, pour over the water, stir and leave for 15 minutes. Fluff up with a fork and stir in the vegetables and mint. Check for seasoning and serve with the salmon.

Chocolate Sorbet (with coffee ice cream, maybe)
For the sorbet:

> 90g/3oz caster sugar
> 300ml/½ pint water plus a further 150ml/¼ pint
> 60g/2oz honey
> 3 heaped tbsps cocoa powder.

In a heavy pan, bring the sugar and 300ml/½ pint water to the boil. Make sure that the sugar is dissolved completely and boil for 2–3 minutes. Stir in the honey and take off the heat. In a separate pan, mix the cocoa to a thin paste with a couple of tablespoons of water taken from the 150ml/¼ pint, and then mix in the rest of the water. Cook for 5 minutes or so, stirring occasionally, then mix in the honey syrup. Freeze in an ice cream maker if you have one, or pour into a shallow plastic container. Freeze until solid, beating from time to time as the mixture freezes, bearing in mind that the more you break up the ice crystals, the tastier it will be. Transfer to the refrigerator to let it soften for about 10–15 minutes before serving. Serve to non-dieters with a scattering of chocolate covered coffee beans, which will also link it nicely to the coffee ice cream if you are intending to serve this as an accompaniment.

Coffee Ice Cream

Obviously, you can buy this, or you can make it a 'let's make a proper egg custard' drama. However, you can perform a marvellous cheat. The egg custard way does taste better, but the cheat's way is good too and you will probably not be caught. This makes slightly more than you will need especially if you are serving it with another ice, but it keeps well. It is particularly good for midnight snacks, because the caffeine keeps you awake so you have to eat more.

Long method:
>   *8 large egg yolks*
>   *150g/5oz golden caster sugar*
>   *300ml/10floz full cream milk*
>   *1 ×284ml carton whipping cream (about 9–10floz)*
>   *1 pinch salt*
>   *1 splash vanilla essence*
>   *2 very very very strong espressos*
>   *instant coffee granules (optional).*

Beat the egg yolks and sugar together in a large heat-proof bowl until pale and thick. Meanwhile, heat the milk, cream, espressos, salt and vanilla together to just under boiling point, and then pour onto the yolks, stirring all the time. Return the mixture back to the heat and heat gently, stirring constantly. Do not let the mixture boil. When it thickens to the consistency of double cream, take it off the heat and park the base of the pan in a sink full of cold water, still stirring. It helps if you have three hands for this manoeuvre. This stops the custard cooking any further. Check for flavour, you may need to beat in a bit of instant coffee and leave to cool completely. Cutting out a circle of carrier bag and pressing it down onto the surface of the custard will prevent a skin forming. When it is completely cold, pour it into the ice cream machine and churn according to instructions, or pour into a Tupperware box and freeze, beating the ice crystals in regularly. Take out of the freezer to soften about 20 minutes ahead of time.

Short version:
>   *2 very very very strong espressos*
>   *1 ×284ml carton whipping cream (about 9–10floz)*

1 ×400g carton bought fresh custard (about 14floz)
extra instant coffee granules, if liked.

Hopefully, you can see where this is going, mix together and freeze.

Pear Shaped Meals

"If an earthquake were to engulf England tomorrow, the English would manage to meet and dine somewhere among the rubbish, just to celebrate the event."

(Douglas Jerrod)

This section has nothing to do with the mould of your Tarte au Poire, but more to do with the fact that occasionally the unthinkable will occur.

If your wits are about you, minor disasters can be taken in your stride. In a hummus recipe if you confuse cloves for bulbs and thus make a garlic purée with a hint of chickpea, do not throw it away. Simply add more beans, fry it up in small balls and label them as garlic patties, serve with yoghurt and mint and a wedge of lemon.

If you keep a well-stocked foodstore, then any one element of a meal can usually be replaced with another. The foodstore is a frontline weapon in crisis management. Watery soup? Pour half of it away, boil it with something with a strong flavour, grill some bread with cheese, put both in a bowl, cover it with the thin soup and call it Mongolian Hot Pot or something that will never be questioned. 'My granny's recipe', is often a good way out, unless granny is one of your guests.

Proportion of Pre-cooked Food

What proportion of pre-cooked and packaged foods is it acceptable to use? This is a question that perplexes many modern hosts. Presumably you do not grow all or indeed any of your own food. Where is the line between serving a supermarket chicken tikka masala, and buying a jar of ready-made curry sauce and adding it to meat and vegetables you have prepared yourself? All food bought at a supermarket is *prepared* to some extent. Indeed, if you can ask a butcher or fishmonger to prepare the meat, fish or fowl, so much the better.

The difficult issues lie in food such as pre-prepared salad bags; vegetable dishes; bought ice cream; meat or fish that has been coated in-store; salmon mousse and pâtés; packet or jar sauce. Garlic mushrooms where the butter is actually in the box with the mushrooms are highly contentious. Shop bought salad dressing. The list is endless and different people believe in differing degrees of acceptability. Many draw the line at buying ready-made punch, but the rule of thumb generally is that a few cheats/shortcuts are acceptable. However, if your main task is to cut open the packaging, place it in the microwave and turn the timer on, where is the fun in that?

Table Talk

> "You'll have no scandal while you dine, but honest talk and wholesome wine"
>
> (Tennyson)

Dinner party conversation is one of the reasons for entertaining. It is good manners for women, seated alternately to men, to talk to the person on their left during the first course, then to the right for the second. The coffee is a chance for alternative parties to chat. A round table changes the dynamic of talking. A guest of honour, if you have one, should not be monopolised. Religion, sex, politics, and the quality of the food should form the staple diet of table talk. Thankfully, the appropriate topics of conversation have changed over the years, so these once taboo subjects will definitely spice up an evening. However, money and illness can still offend and embarrass, so tread carefully.

Chapter 6

Drinks

"I have very poor and unhappy brains for drinking: I could well wish courtesy would invent some other custom of entertainment"

Othello (William Shakespeare)

Unfortunately for Othello, but not for us, drink is very often the life and soul of any party. Although health worries and a need to avoid drinking and driving mean that excesses have to be avoided, drink is still seen as a necessary offering at any party.

Pre-Dinner Drinks

For a pre-dinner drink, champagne is always a winner, as long as it is good quality. There is little sense in serving a bad champagne, when you could obtain an excellent sparkling wine for a similar price. 'Champagne' refers to an area of France and not the type of grape used, and there are sparkling wines made in other places in the same way as champagne. You will be surprised at just how many people are still partial to a glass or several of sherry, particularly before Sunday lunch. Do make sure the sherry you have is not the vile brown 'cream' variety which is only fit for using in trifles – amontillado or fino are good to have to hand. Gin and tonic has declined in popularity but is still the cornerstone of many drinks cabinets. Wine is also perfectly acceptable, though it has to be one that is drinkable on its own; there is no point wasting a good heavy red.

Cocktails serve a purpose and are fun to make and drink. If you are making cocktails, decide on a limited range, or be willing to spend a small fortune on being able to satisfy even the strangest requests. After exhaustive research, we could not find reference to the acceptability of beer as a drink with any stage of a dinner, although it is perfect with a curry. However, there is a great range of beers, lagers, ales, and porters that are available from local breweries and imported from all over the world.

It is also considerate to enquire if your guests do not drink alcohol for any reason. This could be because of religion, abstinence or diet. Attention should never be drawn to the fact unnecessarily as this can seriously embarrass the guest and impose a need to explain the reason, which they may not want to do. It is therefore appropriate to stock up on non-alcoholic beverages. Orange juice is a staple. Home-produced lemonade can offer a quirky semblance of choice. Provide mineral waters, both still and sparkling. Pints of water may often be consumed over the course of a long meal, as well as a full range of alcohol laid on by you, the gracious host. Ensure that there is ice available. In addition, lemon slices make drinks look more attractive.

A useful tip is not to ask your guests what they want with an open question – 'What would you like?' – as you may not have what they ask for. It is better to limit their choices to alternatives such as 'Wine or gin and tonic?'

Drinks During Dinner

Unless you are entertaining a group of teetotallers then wine is the very bedrock of a dinner party. The volume stocked and the type of wine is incredibly important. This is not a wine guide so we will only look at the basics. There are many wine guides available.

These days there is an array of choice available at certain off-licences and wine merchants. There is of course the possibility of a trip to the continent to stock up on inexpensive wines in quantity.

Quality and Quantity

The rule of thumb that one is always told when catering a drinks party is: half a bottle of wine per head. Well. Take on board that rule of thumb, and now disregard it entirely. You know your friends. Will they drink a mere three glasses of wine, or a whole bottle? Use your judgement, and then add at least a couple of bottles for caution's sake. And you can always massively over-order if you have obtained your bottles on a sale or return policy from a local off-licence or wine merchant.

Temperatures

White should be cold, as should champagne. Red Beaujolais is also good cold. A couple of hours in the refrigerator should suffice, although the Wine Society suggest that white wine is being drunk too cold, while red is too warm. Consider the use of wine coolers. Wine can become warm very quickly so devise some method of keeping it cool. A refrigerator is ideal but is often too far away from your glasses. Ice buckets can become messy. The vacuum or terracotta-type cooler can serve a purpose but will not keep the wine cold for much longer than an hour.

Red should be served at room temperature. This actually depends upon the temperature of the room where you are serving it. Open the bottle a couple of hours before you anticipate drinking it. Avoid using the microwave or the oven to warm up wine. Be careful about leaving red wine to stand in the kitchen as it is often prone to warming, especially when a big meal is being prepared.

What Goes with What

If you are not sure if a certain wine will go with a certain meal or particular course, then if possible attempt a dry run of your menu and drink various wines with it. This should be a pleasure in itself. Rules of thumb – dry white wine goes well with fish and seafood. Red wine goes better with meat. Of course a freshly grilled tuna steak is considerably more meaty than an insipid breast of chicken, so use your judgement. A good rosé can be drunk with, say, salmon. Heavy meat, such as game or roast joints of beef or lamb, can take a heavier wine like Burgundy. Lighter dishes may suit lighter reds.

As you may suspect, pudding wines are sweet affairs that can be used to accompany pudding. Sauternes or Muscat are classics and there are also some unpronounceable German dessert wines.

Red wine is generally served in rounder glasses, white in thinner glasses and fizzy in flutes. If you serve fizzy in wide glasses, it loses its fizz more quickly. A wineglass should be wide enough to spin the wine around the circumference of the bowl and thus release the flavour.

If you are planning to serve any mature wines, particularly aged reds, there may be some bottle stink or sediment. It is best to decant these wines slowly through a strainer. This avoids disturbing the sediment. If the wine is acutely past its best then do not let it breathe. Polish it off quickly or simply throw it out!

It is a useful idea to keep information about wine and food combinations, as well as a note of which wine you have served to which guests. Details such as name, year, stockists, and what food you think it would go well with are useful. If you attend wine-tasting evenings more than a few times a year or are a regular gastronome then you will quickly build up a comprehensive reference system. We often find ourselves enjoying a good glass of wine, and some time in the future subsequently fail to remember what it was.

Bringing Wine

It is now quite usual for a guest to bring wine as an offering to the host. If you have planned the food and wine to match exactly then it is acceptable to add the gift bottle to your cellar. If you think that the wine bought is of better quality than the wine you are proposing to serve, then maybe you could add it to the menu at the correct phase of the evening and when you have established its correct temperature.

If the wine is a gift over and above what is considered appropriate for the function you are holding then it would be a shame and a waste to open it there and then. Therefore, if you are lucky enough to receive an obscenely expensive bottle of Château Neuf du Pâpe, then perhaps it is better not to open it. Comment that you would like to save it for the birth of a child or some other special occasion.

Port & Spirits

Pass port clockwise. This is the real essence of port decorum. Keep it going to the left especially if there are service members present, as this is where the tradition originates. Beware of sediment and decant to remove this. Vintage ports should not be served too cold.

Spirits might be required before dinner in the form of cocktails or gin and tonic for example. Heavy-duty drinkers may ask for whisky before dinner too. If whisky is requested, enquire if ice or water is required. In this respect, much depends upon the quality of the whisky.

Coffee

Many prefer strong coffee when served after dinner. It is polite to have decaffeinated available for those who want it. There are several ways of making coffee. Do not offer too many choices. If anyone asks for 'half fat foam, half caffe latte with a whisper of cinnamon', give them filter and a good hard stare. Small chocolates are good at the coffee stage. After Belgian truffles, mints may seem a little pallid but are excellent for digestion and removing the 'sweet' taste from your palette. Serving coffee in a different room to the meal is a wholly personal matter nowadays which may give your guests a welcome chance to talk to someone other than their dinner companions. You must judge whether the evening needs shaking up a little. You could perhaps leave the option to your guests, as they will then move between the two rooms as they wish. If they want to break from the table then this means that you, as the host, may need to wander between the two rooms. At this stage of the evening, you may find it useful to leave bottles of whatever people are drinking in both the dining and drawing room areas.

There is little need to discuss the protocol concerning the exit of all women present while the men continue with the port and cigars. It is hoped that you will be part of the movement that consigns this to the history books.

Smoking

It used to be expected that the host provided a supply of cigarettes for guests. This is not the case nowadays although this might be seen as a thoughtful gesture. It is, however, quite normal to have a supply of cigars if you think that these will be needed and it is correct to do so at a formal dinner. Some cigars need cutting and you will need implements for this. It is better to invest in a cigar cutter or purchase cigars that do not need trimming.

The critical issue about smoking nowadays is whether to allow guests to smoke at all, if you or others in your party do not. This is a tough one. Much depends upon how severe are the attitudes of the anti and pro lobbies assembled. Hopefully you will find that guests will ask permission before smoking. It is a shame that there is not an algorithm where you can calculate the level of smoke comfort using variables such as the number of smokers, the volumetric space and the quality of ventilation. Other computations would include an assessment of the attitude, age and bronchial health of those not smoking.

Consider offence caused to both parties and act accordingly. Satisfaction could be achieved through segregation, by either inviting your smoking and non-smoking friends to different parties, or by allowing the smokers to use the garden and drawing room only, but not the kitchen, or dining room. There is no simple solution. If you do allow smoking, then make sure that there are plenty of ashtrays available, which are emptied frequently. If you want to avoid ash on the crockery, the floor, the television, or the plant pots, it is necessary for an ashtray to be within two arm lengths of any guest at any time. This may sound excessive, but as the evening progresses, the body of a smoker may become less adept at hand eye co-ordination.

Drunks

Most parties pass off without serious drunken incidents. However, it may be your misfortune to have someone present who has imbibed too much at a wholly inappropriate stage of the proceedings. There are a few tips for minimising the impact of overindulgence in alcohol on an evening:

- Do not serve your first course at 10.30 p.m. if your guests have arrived at 7 p.m.
- Deal with the offending drunk as you see fit – the aim here is to minimise mess and embarrassment to him/her, your other guests and yourself
- Do not let them drive home – especially in someone else's car. Call a taxi
- If known for excess, don't invite at all.

There are bound to be certain drunken activities that irritate you and your guests. The typical ones include fighting and pawing. These are not acceptable and the offending guest should be escorted out. Other irritating incidents include food fights, water pistol battles, pouring wine over the floor deliberately and using the carpet as a giant ashtray.

Depending on where you draw the line, and how informal your party is, singing, getting naked, drinking games, falling over, and dancing could all lead to a guest not being asked again.

If usual tactics do not work and there is a real problem with someone being particularly unpleasant then feel free to ask that person(s) to leave. Asking may not be enough, so a taxi or a lift home may be necessary. It may even be appropriate for them to stay the night. Hopefully they will remember just enough to offer their deepest apologies even if they cannot remember the specifics of the situation. The chances of them getting another invite will depend on previous form and their behaviour before becoming drunk.

Chapter 7

Parties

Canapés

To be perfectly honest, the surest way to drive yourself to madness is to cater your own party (and by 'party' I mean anything over about 12 people). The average domestic kitchen simply doesn't have enough space to store all the paraphernalia – glasses, napkins, platters, flower arrangements, Tupperware boxes full of delicious and yet fragile morsels on filo pastry. The most successful party I ever gave was my 29th birthday party last year, and I invited everyone I knew to a carpet picnic. They came to the flat armed with a picnic and some wine, and I provided paper plates, spangly wine, music, birthday cake and rugs on the floor. It was great. No fuss, no hassle – the easiest party I've ever given. I did live off chicken wings and broccoli quiche for three days afterwards, and upon clearing up the flat, I did find a solitary rollmop herring quietly putrefying under the coffee table, which made me sit down rather suddenly. But I highly recommend it as a way of doing parties.

The irony about parties, though, is that everybody adores canapés. They are so easy to eat, there are lots of different and exciting flavours, and they are usually on pastry of some kind, which always gets the vote. But they are so difficult to make in a domestic kitchen, or rather, difficult to make well. And I for one resent the fact that you slave over them for hours, decorating and cutting out tiny shapes and piping curlicues of horseradish cream about the place, and – one bite and they're gone. Also, usually, they are on bases (crostini, or filo pastry tartlets), and this means you have to assemble them at the last minute because otherwise they go soggy. Or they're hot ones, and you're worried that they might burn while you're answering the door to the 800th person. This, in turn, means that you can't enjoy your own party because you are maniacally layering mozzarella onto wafers of ciabatta as the first guests arrive, and having to keep an ear out for the oven timer for the ham and mustard croutes during your riveting conversation with the first wife of your best girlfriend's newest conquest. I suggest buying the whole lot. Oh, and another tip – ignore all those polite 'how many pieces per head' suggestions you get from recipe books or professional party planners. I personally go to parties with the sole intention of eating enough canapés to make it count as supper as well, and you only need two or three people like me at a small drinks party to throw the numbers out completely. And you really do need to serve some form of food at drinks parties. Preferably quite solid food, especially if most of your guests have come from work and will be drinking on empty stomachs. Pizza squares are good, or little hot new potatoes served with a dip made from sour cream, a little bit of chopped fresh dill and some black lumpfish roe (I am not going to insult you by giving you a recipe for that – honestly). Another good idea, if you have enough espresso cups, is to serve little amounts of soup (leek and potato in winter, vichyssoise in the summer – spot the difference) in espresso cups.

My other tip about drinks parties is don't mess about worrying whether to offer people the choice from the drinks cabinet. Keep it simple. Offer them the choice of white (or champagne), red or soft. Bang. Three choices, nothing more. And I don't give people orange juice – it is very acidic and heavy and you can't drink more than about two glasses without feeling a bit bug eyed. This is a purely personal veto, though, because I'm not keen on it and there are invariably cartons and cartons of it left over and all I can think to do with it is make it into Orange Chicken (p. 128) or, of course, how could I forget? Mary's Knees, the most delicious and deceptively easy to drink cocktail in the world. It tastes like you're drinking orange juice, until you try to stand up. And no, I don't know where the name comes from. Anyway, back to other soft options for drinks parties: fizzy mineral water, or cranberry juice, or elderflower cordial diluted with soda, or Aqua Libra (yes! remember that?), or Claire Stewart's great tip, tonic water with a splash of Angostura bitters and lots of ice.

Parties

Mary's Knees
(makes 21 glasses/3½ pints)

>   300ml/10floz vodka
>   150ml/5floz Cointreau or Grand Marnier or other orange liqueur
>   150ml/5floz Campari
>   juice of 2–3 limes
>   1.5l/2½ pints orange juice.

Mix together really well (the Campari will make it go the most beautiful pinky orange colour) and chill. Serve in long glasses over ice in the sunshine.

If you feel you really must make the canapés yourself, you could do the palmiers from p. 51 (*Suppers*), or I've given a couple of ideas for easy but good ones. I quite often do these instead of a first course at dinner parties, especially if I know one or two of the guests are going to be really late. This way, everyone who arrives on time gets something to mop up the excess gin and tonic with, and when Simon hurtles through the door at 9.30p.m. muttering sorry, sorry, you can move directly to the main course without holding up the whole proceeding by having to get everyone to sit down to a tricksy little salad first. This will at least give your friends the option of being home by midnight if they want. I have said these are easy, which they are – but they are also time-consuming. Don't say I didn't warn you.

Crostini with Roasted Green Peppers, Cumin and Black Olives
For the Crostini:

>   1 baguette or ficelle
>   extra virgin olive oil.

Get a baguette or a ficelle (and I have to say, the ficelle makes a better size of crostino – a slice of baguette is just a shade too large. However, the chances of finding a ficelle when you really want one are minimal, so a baguette will do admirably.) If you can have thought ahead so that it's slightly stale, better and better, but it's not vital. Slice it on a slight diagonal about 1–2cm/½–¾ in thick. Turn the oven on to about 180C/Gas 4. Have a wide shallow bowl standing by with about 1cm/½ in extra virgin olive oil in it, and dip both sides of the bread into it quickly – don't let it soak as it will become terribly greasy. Transfer the dipped bread to a shallow baking tray and bake for about 8–12 minutes till nice and golden (keep an eye on them as they go brown very quickly at the end). Cool on a wire rack. You can store these for about a day in a really well-sealed container, but not much longer. You can also, depending on what you intend to put on them, flavour the crostini with other things when you make them – e.g. if you've going to top them with a mixture of creamy blue cheese mashed with a bit of mascarpone, then a bit of walnut oil in the olive oil is good; or if you are doing anything tomatoey then put a bit of garlic in the oil.

This is not a very beautiful crostini topping, but it does taste wonderful.

For the topping:

> *4 green peppers*
> *olive oil*
> *garlic*
> *ground cumin*
> *good quality black olives (not the ready-pitted ones in a tin, please, or the Greek style slightly wrinkled ones which taste of metal).*

Roast and skin the peppers. Try to make sure they are cooked and a bit floppy, and not raw and crunchy. Cut into fine strips and put into a non-metallic bowl. Drizzle with some really good quality olive oil (not too much, just enough to anoint, not so they're sitting in a pool), add one or two crushed cloves of garlic and about a teaspoon of ground cumin. Stone the olives (I use about half a jar, enough to have one olive per bit of bread) and stir all together. Set aside till you're ready to make the crostini, which basically means coiling a few strips of pepper on the croûte, topping with one or two bits of olive (depending on how neatly you've been able to stone them) and putting on a plate. They do look a bit unprepossessing ('green worms', as one guest remarked). Hmmm. You could pretty them up, maybe with a ring of fresh red chilli for colour contrast? Or, you can just serve them and keep quiet. And it has just occurred to me that instead of going through the drama of stoning olives, you could just spread each croute with a thin layer of black olive paste from a jar before topping with the peppers. Got to be a good idea, that.

Cheese Sablés

This comes originally from the Constance Spry Cookery Book, and are so unbelievably easy that once you have made them once you will no longer even need a recipe.

Equal weights of:

> unsalted butter at room temperature
> strong hard cheese (e.g. Cheddar, Parmesan, Gruyère, Red Leicester. Try to avoid using all Cheddar as they do then end up tasting a bit like feet. I like using a mixture of cheeses.)
> plain flour
> a little dried mustard powder
> beaten egg
> fennel seeds, caraway seeds, mustard seeds, toasted sesame seeds, poppy seeds, dried chilli flakes, cumin seeds.

In a food processor, buzz the butter with the cheese, then work in the flour and mustard powder. Check for seasoning (I always add ground black pepper, and usually salt, but be careful with the salt as it will depend on the cheese). Cut open a plastic bag (I am determined that you use them up from that Lakeland Plastics floral tube hanging on the back of the kitchen door) and plop the dough onto the inner side of it. Form it into a rough sausage shape about 3.5–5cm/1½–2in in diameter), roll it up in the plastic and chill until hard. (Tip – if you make extra dough, you can keep it in the freezer and just shave off biscuits for baking as and when you feel like having them. This plays havoc with a calorie-controlled diet.) Line baking sheets with baking parchment, slice biscuit mixture as thinly as possible and transfer to the baking sheet. They spread out slightly, but not hugely. Brush with egg and sprinkle with whichever seeds you fancy (fennel are my favourite but the masses seem to prefer sesame or mustard). Bake at 190C/Gas 5 for 5–10 minutes until golden and slightly puffed. Warning – these biscuits go from raw to burnt in milliseconds, and the minute they are brown rather than golden they develop a really unpleasant bitter taste which even the dog will reject, so watch them like a hawk. And funnily, even in a fan oven, they do better in the top of the oven. Cool on a wire rack. Nicest cold, funnily, not hot. Terrifyingly moreish with gin and tonic.

Buffets

Buffets aren't quite so bad. In fact, if you are feeding anywhere upwards of 14 people, often a buffet is the only way to do it. You can't 'plate up' 14 meals in the kitchen, and the great advantage of a buffet is that the very nature of it dictates that everything has to be ready ahead of time, so it can be arranged on the sideboard or (in our house) the wallpaper pasting table with a cloth on. Buffets are particularly nice in the summer, when people can take their food outside and mill around on the croquet lawn à la Merchant Ivory. Don't try to serve the food outside though – nothing, even food designed for hot weather – looks at its best after two hours of 75°F heat. Jambon persillé – the old French classic of chunks of cooked ham and parsley in aspic – looks very pretty even when it's been attacked by forks, and is easy to make (there are any amount of good recipes out there, from Elizabeth David's onwards, so I won't give one here). Winter buffets are good too – often lunch after a christening, or possibly after a funeral, although if there was ever a time to indulge in getting someone in to do the catering, a wake would be pretty near the top of my list. If the deceased was someone close to you, you'll be in no fit state to cook. This is why you have relatives who can help out. Plus, everyone who has come back to the house will want, at some point over the afternoon, to come and speak to you and offer their condolences, and this will be difficult if you are peering into the oven with a smudge of flour on your nose. Don't be too ambitious with your buffet – nothing fragile or temperature-sensitive, as it will have to sit around for long periods of time while people discuss why Great Uncle Rory wasn't invited to the party, and salmonella is a very real threat to large catered parties. Something like chilli con carne, or shepherd's pie, is brilliant. If you have a chafing dish (and if you do, congratulations, you must be about the only person on the planet outside of an Indian restaurant who does) then now is your big chance – get it out and keep the potatoes warm in it. And finally, don't offer people too many choices. Two or three main dishes maximum (depending on numbers), otherwise people get greedy and pile their plates ridiculously high with a cacophony of flavours which don't go together at all, plus it gets revoltingly messy on the buffet table itself. Try to keep one of the dishes at least super plain to please all palates, for example a cold cooked Bradenham ham is always welcome, and means that you will get fantastic leftovers. I'm not going to insult you by saying things like:

- Green salad
- Potato salad – the best I've ever had had no mayonnaise in it but was dressed with half vinaigrette, half crème fraîche and lots and lots of chopped fresh herbs and spring onions
- Rice salad
- Pasta salad
- Garlic bread
- Baked potatoes.

Obvious, obvious, obvious. Just please, please don't make coleslaw. I hate it. Especially with raisins in. And one more thing – this is not intended to be an entire menu, just a selection of ideas for you. I haven't given pudding ideas because there are so many good ones you could do – cheesecakes, or trays of brownies, or individual meringues, or fruit salad, or apple pie – it does rather depend on what has gone before. Fruit jellies are good in summer as long as you can keep them cool. Obviously don't serve soufflés, but chocolate mousse always goes down well.

Summer Buffet
Salmon Koulibiac
Three Colours Red Chicken Skewers
Baked Courgettes with Tomato and Parmesan
Green Beans with Ham and Tomato

Salmon Koulibiac
(makes enough for 2 tarts)

I refer you to p. 132 for the theory behind these quick tart cases. Just make sure you have enough pastry and enough filling, and you can keep these coming – no problem. They're also good cold (or at room temperature).

> 2 ×375g packs of ready-rolled puff pastry, cooked as described on p. 132 to make large vol au vent cases
> just over 1kg/2½ lbs salmon fillet, skinned (or, if you are on a budget, use equivalent tinned tuna, and add a few capers to the mixture)
> 500ml/1pt stock
> 175g/6oz basmati or brown rice
> 125g/4oz butter
> 4 fat leeks, sliced
> 250g/8oz mushrooms, thickly sliced
> 2–3 tbsps freshly chopped dill
> 2–3 tbsps chopped fresh parsley
> juice and rind 2 lemons
> 4–6 hard-boiled eggs, roughly chopped
> 125g/4oz hollandaise sauce or more, to bind (and I will, for once, let you use the stuff in a jar, because you're mixing it with so many other ingredients that it's not so crucial to have homemade).

Lightly poach the fish in the stock, taking care not to overcook (as you're going to heat it through again later), then drain and flake, reserving the stock, which you should now use to cook the rice. Fry the leeks and mushrooms in the butter till soft, and then mix all the ingredients together. Add more hollandaise if you think it needs it. Check for seasoning – you will need to add lots of freshly ground black pepper and some salt – and you might need more lemon. Fill the pastry cases and bake at 180C/Gas 4 for about 10 minutes, just to let the ingredients settle. Serve, scattered with more dill.

Three Colours Red Chicken Skewers

These are great because they make portion control dead easy. This amount makes 8–10 skewers. If you want to make these vegetarian, substitute Halloumi cheese for the chicken.

> 8 skinless chicken breasts
> 3 red peppers, in chunks

2 red onions, cut into wedges
2 tbsps balsamic vinegar
4 tbsps flavourless oil
2 red chillies, chopped
1–2 cloves garlic, crushed
1 small bunch spring onions, chopped
2 tbsps chopped fresh basil
salt and pepper.

In a non-metallic bowl mix the vinegar, oil, chillies, garlic, spring onions, basil and seasoning and marinate the chicken for up to 6 hours. Thread onto skewers alternately with the onion and pepper and grill or bake for 10–15 minutes, basting with the marinade, until done. Good hot or cold. These are also excellent on the barbecue.

Baked Courgettes with Tomato and Parmesan
(serves 6–8 as a side dish)

1 aubergine, in 2cm/1in cubes
3–4 fat courgettes (or equivalent in smaller courgettes), in 2cm/1in chunks
4 plum tomatoes or 20 or so cherry tomatoes, coarsely chopped (don't chop the cherry tomatoes, obviously)
2–3 cloves garlic, crushed
about a third of a baguette, cut into 2cm/1in cubes
2 tbsps fresh chopped parsley
couple of tbsps extra virgin olive oil
4 or more tbsps freshly grated Parmesan.

Toss all except the Parmesan together in a bowl and season well. Tip into an oiled china baking dish (those glazed terracotta ones are good), drizzle with another tablespoon or so of oil, sprinkle over the Parmesan and bake at 190C/Gas 5 for about half an hour, till the vegetables are just beginning to catch on top and the chunks of bread that you can see are golden and crusty. This is perfect for buffets as it is actually better warm than piping hot. Also good as a side dish for roast lamb with flageolet beans.

Green Beans with Ham and Tomato
1kg/2lb green beans, topped and tailed

> 2 tbsps olive oil
> 2 onions, finely chopped
> 2 cloves garlic, crushed
> 120–200g/4–6oz parma ham or smoky bacon, chopped
> small tin tomatoes.

Cook the beans till al dente (steaming is good), then refresh under cold running water. Fry the onion in the olive oil, then add the ham and garlic and cook for 2–3 minutes. Add the tomatoes and reduce till nice and thick (about 10 minutes). Check for seasoning (nutmeg is quite nice too if you like it). Stir in the beans and serve hot or at room temperature.

Winter Buffet

Garlic Mushrooms
Lamb Tagine with Prunes
Turkey, Tomato and Ricotta Lasagne
Gratin Dauphinois

Garlic Mushrooms

This is sort of halfway between a starter and a side dish, and is peculiarly useful for buffets – it can be used as an emergency baked potato filling for the vegetarian you forgot about, in which case call it Mushroom Stroganoff, or as a bulker-outer of main courses if it looks like you're running out of food. Also, it could not be easier.

> 2lbs field mushrooms, thickly sliced
> 4 cloves garlic, crushed
> 6oz butter, melted
> 4 tbsps chopped fresh parsley
> 170ml/6floz double cream
> salt, pepper, nutmeg.

Mix all together and bake in a ceramic dish for about 20–25 minutes, stirring once or twice.

Lamb Tagine with Prunes

To be strictly authentic you must make tagine in one of those conical dishes from Tangiers. Yeah, right. I make mine in a non-stick Tefal casserole dish and no-one has ever, ever gainsaid me. Last time I made this I served it for Sunday lunch and used 18 neck fillets. There were nine people at the table, of whom two were vegetarian, and there was not a speck of lamb left. Do I have greedy friends? Is this exceptionally delicious? Were the neck fillets peculiarly small? Your call. All I'm saying is, make lots. You won't be sorry. I also – and this is definitely not authentic – made this with prunes that had been soaking in Armagnac, just because I had so many jars of them that I was worried I was never going to use up them any other way. You should make this a day in advance, because lamb is quite fatty and it's nice to be able to skim off the excess fat. Also, all casseroles benefit from being made in advance, and this one more than most.

> 18 neck fillets of lamb (which really should be far too much meat) but I suppose there are no bulking vegetables in this. A normal quantity of lamb would be about 2kg/4½ lbs for about eight people. You can also use shoulder, or leg. Cut it into large (4cm/1½ in cubes)
> flavourless oil
> 4 red onions, chopped
> 4 cloves garlic, crushed
> tsp cayenne
> tsp dried ginger
> tsp ground cumin
> 1–2 dried chillies or 1 chopped fresh red chilli
> heaped tsp cinnamon or a couple of cinnamon sticks
> 3 bay leaves
> 3 tbsps coarsely crushed black peppercorns
> tbsp turmeric
> 4 tbsps runny honey (or equivalent stiff)
> 2 ×400g chopped tinned tomatoes
> squeeze tomato purée
> grated rind and juice 1 orange
> packet fresh coriander, coarsely chopped, stems, roots and all
> 500g/1lb prunes, ready to eat if you can get them, or dried is fine too
> another packet coriander, to serve.

Brown the lamb in batches in a pan big enough to hold it all, and set aside. In the same pan, gently brown the onion, then stir in the garlic, herbs and spices and stir around till fragrant. Return the lamb to the pan and add the honey, tomatoes, orange, chopped coriander and enough water to cover. (I sometimes add a bit of red wine, or a stock cube at this stage.) Bring to the boil, cover and simmer for about 45 minutes. Add the prunes and cook for a further 15 minutes, keeping an eye on the liquid if you are using unsoaked prunes (and you are undercooking at this stage as you are going to reheat it tomorrow and you don't want the meat to completely disintegrate). Fish the meat out with a slotted spoon (or more often, I pour the whole thing into a colander). Chill, separately, overnight, and skim off the – abundant – fat from the surface of the sauce. Reheat the lamb in the sauce – check for seasoning – and just before serving chop the remaining coriander, stir in about half and scatter the rest over the surface. Good with couscous.

Turkey, Tomato and Ricotta Lasagne

(makes one lasagne to serve eight as part of a buffet)
For the sauce:

2 large onions, chopped
8–12 rashers smoked streaky bacon, chopped
4 cloves garlic, crushed
2 carrots, chopped
2 sticks celery, chopped
1 red pepper, chopped
olive oil
2 ×tins chopped tomatoes
250ml/8floz red wine
2 tbsps chopped fresh basil
³/₄ tsp dried thyme or oregano or herbes de Provence
1 tsp dried red pepper flakes
750g/1½ lb cooked turkey meat, in chunks.

Fry the onion, bacon, garlic, carrots, celery and pepper in the olive oil till softening, then add the tomatoes, wine, herbs and pepper flakes. Bring to the boil then reduce slightly (don't forget, the pasta will absorb a lot of moisture). Stir in the turkey.

> 500g/1lb Ricotta cheese or, to be honest, you could use cottage cheese
> 1 large egg, beaten
> 1 bunch spring onions, chopped
> packet ready-to-use lasagne sheets
> 500g/1lb Mozzarella, grated
> 30g/1oz Parmesan, grated.

In a bowl mix together the Ricotta, egg and spring onion. Season. Layer a third of the tomato sauce on the bottom, then a layer of pasta, then half the Ricotta, then half the Mozzarella, then another layer of pasta, then another third of the sauce, then the remaining Ricotta, then a layer of pasta, then top with the rest of the sauce and sprinkle the remaining Mozzarella on top, and finally the Parmesan. Cover with foil and bake at 180C/Gas 4 for 30 minutes, then remove the foil and bake for another 10–15 minutes till top is bubbling and golden.

Gratin Dauphinois

People love these potatoes. They are full of delicious unhealthy cream, so people never get them at home. They go brilliantly with cold meat and also with stews. Vegetarians can eat them. They taste better warm than searing hot. They are easy to make. How much more persuading do you need? Makes enough for 8–12 as a side dish.

> 1.5kg/3lb potatoes, ideally waxy but I can guarantee no-one will complain
> 1.5l/3pts milk
> 900ml/1½ pts double cream
> salt, pepper, nutmeg
> 2 cloves garlic, crushed.

Peel the potatoes and slice them thinly. In the ideal world you would plunge the slices into a basin of cold water to wash off the excess starch but frankly I have never bothered. In a buttered dish (or two or three, depending on the size of your dishes) layer the slices, seasoning each layer with salt and pepper. In a jug mix the cream, milk, garlic and nutmeg and pour it over the potatoes. Bake at 160C/Gas 3 for about 1½ hours. Turn up the heat at the end if the top layer hasn't gone crusty and golden.

Chapter 8

House Parties

I'm going to tell you now that this particular chapter is, as far as I am concerned, a bit of a con. I live in a two bedroom flat in Fulham and let's face it, I am never going to give a house party here. I am drawing on experience gained from being a guest at other people's house parties, which I have been doing for a while now and think I'm quite good at. So settle back and enjoy the fiction.

It is an utter fallacy that lasagne is an easy option. Frying mince, making white sauce, blanching pasta strips – I'm sorry, but nothing that dirties four pans before you even get it into the oven can be good news. If one of your guests volunteers to bring it with them, jump at the chance (and I would go so far as to specify a particularly delicious smoked fish lasagne which I found in a magazine recently – it is hell to make, but truly delicious to consume). Just don't put yourself through the agony – you will be cross and hot and in no mood to sparkle at guests.

The answer to having people for the weekend is, and I'm sorry if you want to hit me for repeating myself, Plan Ahead. If you know you've got eight people arriving on Friday night at various times from various parts of the country, for the sake of your sanity you must make something which will not spoil if it is kept waiting by the lorry fire on the M3 corridor. This means no soufflés, no pastry, no roasts. It does mean, on the other hand, big warming casseroles (if winter), or a stir fry (so you chop up all the bits ahead of time and then just cook them at the last minute), or pasta (where you can make the sauce ahead and just keep everyone quiet with a large drink and some olives while you take 10 minutes to boil up the rigatoni).

Saturday breakfast can and should be an uncomplicated affair – I would suggest toast and marmalade and cereal, no startling departures from form – because generally Saturdays people want to be up and out – going racing, or shopping, or even just for a walk. Saturday lunch either should be out in a little country pub you've discovered, or a table picnic – lots of cold meat and cheese and salad (i.e. minimum effort). If you want to look as if you've tried a bit harder than opening packets, boil some potatoes, or make some garlic bread, or make the Indian Potatoes below. Also, people do often like a 'finishing point' to picky lunches like this, otherwise the danger is that one continues to nibble for hours after one is essentially full – so it's an idea to have a counterpoint to all the little inviting plates of duck sausage and olives and what have you. Maybe produce a fantastic piece of really good cheese, or even a proper pudding – apple tart, or sticky caramel upside down cake. Saturday supper will probably be a dinner party, to which you may have invited some local friends, and on Sunday you will probably only manage two meals – the enormous breakfast (see comments above on brunch) and Sunday lunch.

Ahhh, Sunday lunch with friends. As you will know from the chapter on lunches, in my opinion Sunday lunch is just about the most stressful thing you can do. More confessions of a real life cook here – I hate making roasts. Actually, that's not strictly true. The roast itself is a doddle. Anoint meat with flavourings and park in oven for required time. Couldn't be easier. What WILL give you a stress frenzy, however, is the timing of the accompanying vegetables. I defy anybody to remain calm when they are faced with making Yorkshire puddings and roast potatoes simultaneously, bearing in mind that the oven will already have one shelf taken up with an enormous piece of beef. Never mind that you are also madly cooking roast parsnips, broccoli, leeks in white sauce, cauliflower cheese and gravy. Dirtying every pan in the kitchen in the process. Why do it to yourself? This weekend is supposed to be fun. How can it be fun when you're making yourself ill with worry about flaked almonds for the green beans?

So at the risk of annoying you all with my unvarying chant, Do It Ahead. Or at least, do most of it ahead, and only leave yourself the last minute bits. What about a chicken, rubbed with olive oil, lemon and cumin, then plainly roasted, using the hot pan juices as a salad dressing? Or cold rare roast beef? Or just a simple leg of lamb with vegetables? Depending on the weather, do ice cream, or make a steamed pudding, or a tray of brownies, or some really good cheese and fruit. It's largely up to you to gauge how traditional your friends are feeling for Sunday lunch.

Suggested Ideas
Chinese Pork
Indian Potatoes
Apple, Date, Ginger and Garlic Chutney
Sticky Upside Down Cake

Chinese Pork

>1 chicken stock cube
>170ml/6floz hot water
>1 tbsp cornflour
>1 tbsp black treacle
>1 tsp soy sauce
>½ tsp salt
>flavourless oil, e.g. groundnut
>1 large onion, cut into wedges
>500g/1lb pork fillet, thinly sliced
>1 green pepper, in strips
>1 small can water chestnuts, sliced
>handful cashew nuts.

Dissolve the stock cube in the water, then add the cornflour, treacle, soy and salt. Set aside till needed. Brown the onion in very hot oil, add the meat and brown. Add pepper; cook for 1 minute then add water chestnuts. Add the stock and stir constantly until thickened. Sprinkle over the cashew nuts, and serve at once with rice.

Indian Potatoes

A word of warning – the turmeric in this stains terribly, so be sure to put on an apron. With thanks to Caroline Priestley for this.

>960g/2lbs cold boiled potatoes (in their skins) – you can use leftovers or do them specially
>15g/½ oz butter
>splash flavourless oil

> 1 dessertsp turmeric
> 1 level dessertsp sesame seeds
> 2 tsps black mustard seeds
> 1 heaped tsp fennel seeds
> salt and pepper.

Cut the potatoes into chunks and fry in the oil and butter with the turmeric. When beginning to brown, add the rest of the spices. Fry till crusty, season to taste and serve. Really delicious with cold roast pork.

Apple, Date, Ginger and Garlic Chutney

This is dead easy to make (except I warn you, the house will smell like a pickle factory for about a day, and, also, it does take at least a month to mature, so you should make it in advance). Quantities are approximate only; if you use 175g/6oz sultanas instead of 350g/12oz, it really doesn't matter that much. It is sensational with cold ham and also with creamy Vignottes.

> 1kg/2lbs apples (cooking apples are best, or Granny Smiths, otherwise the chutney is just too sweet)
> 500g/1lb dates, stoned and chopped
> 1.5kg/3lb onions, peeled and sliced
> 2 whole heads garlic, peeled and crushed
> 125g/4oz chopped fresh ginger or crystallised ginger or stem ginger in syrup
> 700g/$1\frac{1}{2}$ lb sugar (brown or white)
> $\frac{1}{2}$ tsp cayenne
> 2 tsps salt
> 1 tsp dry English mustard powder
> 1/$1\frac{1}{2}$ pints cider vinegar.

Chop all fruits and vegetables, put into a large pan with remaining ingredients, bring to the boil then simmer and cook, uncovered, for about two hours till thick and much darker in colour. Warning – you must, must crush the garlic not chop it. The first time I made this I thought I would just chop it finely. Big mistake. The rest of the chutney went a lovely rich brown, and the little tiny cubes of garlic stayed white like toenail clippings. It was not a good effect. Bottle in warmed sterilised glass jars, seal and store in a dark cool place for at least a month till ready.

Sticky Upside Down Cake

This is fab. And you can use it on many occasions. Dress it up with cream for a pudding, or downplay it for teatime. Use maple syrup if you are feeling extravagant, instead of caramel. Use any fruits you like. Some good combinations are:

- Sliced pears (and you can add some chopped crystallised ginger to the caramel)
- Slices of orange and banana
- Apricot halves
- Apple
- Rhubarb.

I could go on. But here's the method instead. You will need a deep-sided 24cm/9in cake tin. Line the base of the tin with silicon paper and butter it well.
For the topping:

> *175g/6oz sugar*
> *125ml/4floz water.*

Stir the sugar and water together over a low heat till the sugar dissolves, then boil hard till it goes a light golden brown. Pour onto the buttered silicon paper and arrange your fruit of choice on top, remembering that it'll be turned over when it's served.

Set the oven to 190C/Gas 5 and make the cake. It is basically your everyday all-in-one Victoria sponge recipe with some ground almonds substituted for some of the flour (so, if you suddenly realize you don't have any ground almonds, don't worry, just add an equivalent amount of flour). Everything must be at room temperature, and even then the mixture may well curdle. Don't worry – it doesn't affect the flavour.
For the cake:

> *175g/6oz butter*
> *175g/6oz caster sugar*
> *150g/5oz self raising flour*
> *30g/1oz ground almonds*

pinch salt
1 tsp baking powder
3 eggs
grated rind and juice of 1 orange (optional).

Blast the whole lot together in a blender, pour over the fruit and bake for 45–50 minutes till a skewer inserted comes out clean. Cool briefly (not more than 10 minutes) before running a sharp knife round the edge and turning out onto a plate. The caramel goo will run down the sides of the cake onto the plate.

Chapter 9

Cooking in the Open Air

Barbecues

The community spirit is anchored in this form of cookery. With barbecues, you should consider the positioning of the actual grill, wind direction, and location of the neighbours' washing line. Also worth pondering is how many men will wish to prod and play with the food while wearing the apron and chef's hat. The safety of small children should be considered at all times. Provide plenty of napkins, non-shatter glasses and perhaps supply the apparatus to play a game of swingball as games can make for a successful barbecue as it helps take the guests' attention away from how the barbecue is progressing. Dress should always be casual.

Barbecues are great fun, but there is the tendency to say 'oh come over, we're just doing a barbecue'. Well, yes. If you're the man of the house, all you have to do is stand there and put red meat on fire. It brings out the cave man in all of them, apron and tongs notwithstanding. Meanwhile, the woman of the house is driving herself to an early grave making baked potatoes, grilling red peppers for vegetarians, checking paper plates, assembling chutneys, sauces and marinades, par-cooking chickens so the guests don't all contract salmonella, checking there's enough fruit for the Pimms, making green salad, slicing cucumbers – you get the picture. Don't ever make the mistake of thinking a barbecue is the easy option.

I would say make it as simple as possible and don't serve more than two or three main course options: sausages are simply *de rigueur* and lamb chops are always good, as lamb is a nice fatty meat which doesn't dry out. For a more elaborate dish you could cook a whole, butterflied leg of lamb (get your butcher to do the complicated butterflying for you). Cheat a little by partially roasting it in the oven before you start to cook it – this means that you won't all still be standing there ravenous at 5p.m. watching the dwindling embers manfully trying to heat through an enormous joint that has surely come from the biggest lamb on the planet. Also good are spare ribs – and if you can get the long, American cut ones (not the shorter ones that you see in Chinese restaurants), then so much the better. Chicken drumsticks or thigh portions are better than breasts (not so dry). Chicken is particularly good in a yoghurt-based tandoori marinade. It is worth investigating the ranges of ready-made barbecue marinades available in supermarkets these days, even if just for inspiration. It's not hard to sling together the marinades below, but if you are feeling stressed and time is tight then don't let anyone tell you you can't reach for a bottle. (In more ways than one.)

If you want to do fish, I would recommend using a good oily fish: mackerel, if you like it, or red mullet, or for complete luxury a whole sea bass. Sardines are always good, especially if you stuff the stomach cavity with parsley, garlic and lemon before grilling. If you cook fish often on the barbecue, it is really worth investing in one of those fish-shaped 'clamps', which makes turning the critters over so easy. Large shrimps are fantastic on the barbecue (simply marinate in olive oil with masses of chopped garlic and parsley and perhaps some chopped red chilli, and serve with mayonnaise), and one of my favourite things is barbecued lobster. As you can imagine, I don't get to eat it very often. Vegetarians are also easy to cater for – slices of pepper, aubergine or courgette, mushrooms stuffed with blue cheese (see p. 126), or skewers made with cubes of Halloumi cheese (which keeps its shape very well as it grills, making it ideal for barbecuing), peppers and onions, marinated in olive oil and lime juice. Corn on the cob is also excellent on the barbecue, as the charring brings out a really wonderful smoky sweetness in the kernels. It is great served with a chilli, lime and coriander butter.

For puddings on the barbecue, the only things I would wholeheartedly recommend are marshmallows. Pink or white, on a skewer, everyone cooks their own till the outside is black and blistering and the inside is molten gooey sugar. Have ice-cubes standing by for those who burn their tongue on the hot skewer. There is the theory that bananas, baked in their skins, are good, but I tend to find they just go into a dark brown mush. Which is fine if you like that, but I think it's nicer just to produce some proper ice lollies or good ice cream from the freezer (and it's one less thing for you to think about).

Ma Kirkpatrick's Barbecue Sauce

This is so ludicrously easy you won't believe how delicious it tastes. Use to marinate chicken, spare ribs, pork chops, sausages – anything meaty you can sling on a charcoal grill (I think it's a bit strong for fish). Also, it is very good if you are just going to bake something in the oven. Again, it's a question of ratio. I use a mug for measuring this out. The amount given will generously cover enough meat for six.

> 1 mug tomato ketchup
> ¾ mug water
> ¼ mug lemon juice
> ¼ mug Worcestershire sauce.

Tip here: rinse out the tomato ketchupy mug with the water. Combine, pour over meat, set aside for as long as you have, then bake or barbecue till done. Serve with plain boiled rice and chopped fresh parsley.

A slightly – but only just – more elaborate barbecue sauce now.

Hot Honey Mustard Barbecue Sauce

> 1 mug runny honey
> ¾ mug Dijon mustard
> 2–3 tbsps Tabasco
> 1 tbsp soy sauce
> 2 cloves garlic, crushed.

Combine. Pour over meat.

Peach, Orange and Basil Barbecue Sauce

As elaborate as it gets.

> 4 ripe fresh peaches or nectarines, peeled and stoned
> 250ml/8floz dry white wine
> 250ml/8floz orange juice
> 3 tbsps soy sauce
> 1 large bunch fresh basil, chopped

2cm/1in chunk fresh ginger, grated
2 tsps brown sugar.

Buzz together in a blender to break down the peaches, then pour over meat. Particularly nice with pork chops or chicken.

Chili, Lime and Coriander Butter for Corn

This butter is also excellent with roasted sweet potatoes.

125g/4oz softened butter
grated rind 1 lime
½ small red chilli, de-seeded and finely chopped
2 tbsps chopped fresh coriander
salt.

Beat together with a fork. Check for seasoning. Pack into a ramekin and refrigerate till needed.

Coriander Salsa

This keeps well in the fridge for up to a week and is particularly good with grilled steak or lamb chops. It is worth warning your guests that it is terrifically garlicky.

1 whole head fresh garlic
1 red onion
5 large ripe tomatoes
large bunch fresh coriander
1–2 green chillies (or to taste)
125ml/4floz olive oil
90ml/3floz red wine vinegar
salt.

Peel the garlic cloves and the onion. Skin the tomatoes by putting them in a bowl and covering them with boiling water. Wait for one minute, then drain and peel off the skins. Slice them in half and remove the pips. (Ahem. This would be the smart way to do it, but to be perfectly honest, more often than not, I just chop the whole tomato, skin, seeds and all, although I am maniacal about removing the little stalky 'plug' at the top end.) De-seed the chillies. Chop all ingredients finely, either by hand or in the food processor (careful you don't puree them to mush) then combine with the oil and vinegar. It will take quite a bit of salt.

Alfresco

An alternative to cooking outside is the option of eating outside while cooking in a more controlled environment. If you are having many people to dine then you should work with the idea of it being a buffet. To ensure that your guests are kept at the correct temperature too, have some spare jumpers and hot or cold drinks available depending upon how the weather chooses to behave. If it is hot then always provide sunblock for your guests.

Picnics

Sometimes I wonder whether this is supposed to be fun. You're outside, half way up a hill, possibly in the rain, certainly in a cloud of midges, having walked several miles, nowhere to pee in private – and you've had to carry your lunch this far. Hmmm. The picnic. A difficult – but not impossible – concept to a town dweller such as myself. I quite like them, on the whole, but I like them my way. There was the Carpet Picnic I gave for my birthday last year. Or the picnic I went to in Green Park which ended in the most violent downpour and thunderstorm London had seen in 15 years (and me in my flowery shorts running past the Ritz holding a vat of potato salad laughing at the doorman).

Most picnics are dictated by (a) weather – sunny or rainy; and (b) form – are we at a point-to-point, or on a walk? If you're at a point-to-point, or in the car park at Twickenham, you will be able to be a little more extravagant than if you've just climbed vertically up the Campsie Hills lugging all that you intend to eat on your back. This is because you will have the boot of the Range Rover stuffed full of goodies. You are still slightly circumscribed by being in the open air and having to stand round in a circle rather than sit at a table, but you have a certain leeway. Whereas, if you take a picnic on a walk, you're into the realm of weight restriction. You may only eat what you can carry. At its most basic, this can mean simply a packet of sandwiches and an apple. No crockery, no cutlery, no bulky boxes of cake, no knives and forks, no frozen items.

Entertaining and sport seem to share a symbiotic relationship. Events of the status of Henley and Wimbledon have become part of the corporate as well as the social scene. However, the most highbrow of these has elements in common with certain middlebrow events. Glyndebourne and Glastonbury are much the same except for the size of the tents and the volume of the music.

Ensuring the weather is right is very much a part of the British psyche and can mar many picnics. No one likes a cramped car trip to a cold and desolate field or beach, downwind of a slag heap or nuclear recycling facility. The idea of an English picnic evokes an image of tartan rugs, wicker baskets full of all sorts of savouries and sweets, and sitting in a sunny meadow making daisy chains. Somehow the weather always seems to burst this bubble.

At some of the main summer events, including Glyndebourne and Royal Ascot, unless someone is feeding you or you have professional catering, you will need to rustle up a picnic. Summer events are the only ones when there is any real prospect of sitting outside for long enough to eat a slice of Battenburg cake without your fingers dropping off. Picnics are recommended at the following events:

Glyndebourne

A great picnicking venue is Glyndebourne, where picnics are duty bound to be on the prodigal Edwardian scale. Never mind rugs, we want deckchairs, tables, awnings, candelabra, plateaux de fruits de mer, fingerbowls, music. Everyone tries to outdo one another at Glyndebourne with extra touches of lavishness. Corporate hospitality and the new arena give the impression of a more polished event than it once was. Dinner jackets and evening dress are required for these events. Beware, the temperature can fall, even in high summer.

If you are going to go to town, you are going to go to town. Either you get Fauchon to make you up individual hampers – darling – or you take food that is so ridiculously unsuited to picnicking that it becomes part of the challenge. Take things that you have to serve individually – cocottes, ramekins. Things you need special implements for – mussels, lobsters, crabs. Things that are temperamentally unsuited to waiting around – soufflés, elaborate pastry confections. Strew velvet cushions on the damp grass, have a Russian samovar waiting for cups of tea. Give yourself a complete nervous breakdown.

Or, steer into the middle ground. Luxurious but not ridiculous. If you like it (and can afford it), caviar to start. Or if you like it and really can afford it, don't have anything else, just have caviar – a serious amount of it – and then maybe some raspberries.

Picnics are eaten during the 'Long Interval' in the gardens or in the marquee. There is a tradition of informal picnics so bringing in a synod of cooks is not acceptable. As well as keeping the spirit of the event intact, it allows Glyndebourne to sell pre-packed picnic baskets, complete with a porter to lug the food and all the correct implements to your pitch. You will not need to supply your own seats if you are having a picnic outside.

Rugby Internationals

Away trips to Murrayfield for the Six Nations tournament involve a breakfast picnic on the train with fizz and smoked salmon. After taking lunch in a hotel, you can burn off breakfast with the walk to the ground.

Unlike American Football where there are tailgate barbecues in the car park, at Twickenham, a picnic can be eaten in the back of the car, sometimes after having lunched in Richmond. It is important to wear shoes designed for walking. There is a predominance of Barbours or Drizabones. Kilts are sometimes worn by Scots.

Cricket

If you get into the Pavilion at Lords, having been invited, then dress is jacket, trousers, shirt and tie. Food is available at the ground and in the beer tents. This is not really the place to take a rug, as you will have to find somewhere to put it, and the large piece of green flat ground in front of you has another purpose. Some food will be needed though as you will have to have something to do in the rain.

Walking Picnic

Whether it's hot or not, there is nothing like walking up hills to give a person an appetite. People eat much more outside than you would believe. I think that we believe barging up one

Cooking in the Open Air

hill entitles us to wolf down enough protein for three. For really good picnics involving a decent range of food, there need to be at least six bearers. Soup, sandwiches, fruit, chocolate, Bloody Marys, water. One item each to carry. Thank you to Sally Henry for the best picnic of my life, involving all of the above and a view across the Campsie Fells on a clear blue Scottish day that brought us to our knees (or that might just have been the vertical climb it took to get there. Or the effect of the Bloody Marys on an empty stomach.)

Tomato, Butterbean and Pesto Soup

> 3 nice fat leeks, sliced
> 4 large carrots, chopped
> 4 courgettes, chopped
> olive oil
> 750ml/1½ pints stock
> 1 400g/14oz tin chopped tomatoes
> 2 large cans butterbeans, rinsed and drained
> bay leaf
> 2–3 tbsps pesto.

Fry the leeks, carrots and courgettes gently in the olive oil till beginning to soften. Add the stock, tomatoes, beans and bay leaf, and season with a bit of salt and lots of black pepper. Bring to the boil, cover and simmer for 30 minutes, till the vegetables are cooked through. Purée some or all of the soup (depending on desired consistency), return to the pan, stir in pesto to taste and decant into the waiting thermos. Delicious out of mugs on a freezing day.

Smoked Salmon Sandwiches

It is utterly, totally pointless having namby weedy sandwiches when you are so hungry you could eat a scabby-headed dog. Get a proper loaf – granary for preference, as it's more substantial – and carve thick slices. Butter thinly and fill with a really generous amount of smoked salmon. Not just so that there's a little pink smear when you bite into it, but several thick slices. Bit of lemon juice, masses of black pepper. Don't cut the crusts off. Such affectation. Do, however, cut the sandwiches into quarters (squares, please, not triangles). Somehow you can eat more of these small chunky squares than you can of chunky rectangles. Another old picnic favourite – very Enid Blyton – is the hard-boiled egg. Give everybody one as they leave the house, with a screw of paper containing a mixture of salt and black pepper. Brilliant.

Fruit

Tangerines and apples are the best. Bananas are too easily crushed; pears too easily bruised. Cherries are nice but not very substantial. Cherry tomatoes, on the other hand, are inspired, as they are nice and sharp and also quite thirst-quenching.

Chocolate

Those mini, fun-size bars are ideal. Get lots of different kinds and take them all. Or Club biscuits, or Penguin biscuits, if you like them. Or a great slab of Bournville (even for people who profess only to like milk chocolate), if it's not so hot that it will melt in your pocket. Or Kendal mint cake. Or, if you've got sufficiently large pockets to stow at least a small Tupperware box, flapjacks. World's easiest recipe follows.

Flapjacks

>   90g/3oz butter
>   60g/2oz soft brown sugar
>   2 tbsps golden syrup
>   175g/6oz rolled porridge oats
>   pinch salt
>   90g/3oz chopped dates (or chopped apricots, or hazelnuts, or you can leave them out altogether).

Melt butter with sugar and syrup and stir in oats, salt and dates. Pat into an 18cm/7in shallow tin and bake at 180C/Gas 4 for about 20 minutes, till golden brown. Cut into fingers while still warm but leave to cool in the tin.

Car Boot Picnic

Even though you have the luxury of a car boot which will amplify your capacity somewhat, I would still advise against things that need to be eaten from plates. Why bother? You can do that often enough at home. Substantial finger food should be the key here. Crudités with dips, for example – little Gem wedges with a Caesar salad type dressing, perhaps, or bunches of pink radishes. The dukkah from the *Supper* chapter. Scotch eggs (love them or loathe them). Cold sausages, chicken drumsticks. Sandwiches made with creamy soft scrambled eggs piled into a brown bap with lots of crispy streaky bacon piled on top and squashed down with the lid of the bap. Black coffee. Cherry brandy. Sloe gin. Ginger beer.

Pesto Quiche

Actually you needn't make this as quiche, it's just as nice made as a frittata and baked in a buttered ovenproof dish without the pastry. Serve cut into thick wedges with whole cos lettuce leaves to hold them in (saves on plates) and some cherry tomatoes for colour contrast. This is good warm or cold.

> *23cm/9in short-crust pastry case, baked blind – optional*
> *knob of butter*
> *1 onion, finely chopped*
> *90–120g/3–4oz cottage cheese or Ricotta*
> *3 eggs, beaten*
> *170ml/6floz milk*
> *2–3 tbsps pesto*
> *2–3 tbsps grated Parmesan.*

Fry the onion in the butter till translucent. Mix together the cottage cheese, eggs, milk and pesto. Add the onions. Check for seasoning. Pour into the case (if using, or into a buttered dish if not) and bake at the top of the oven at 180C/Gas 4 for about 40 minutes. Scatter the Parmesan over the surface about 10 minutes before the end of cooking time.

Lemon Honey Chicken

> *4 chicken portions (2 drumsticks = 1 portion)*
> *flour seasoned with paprika, salt and black pepper*
> *flavourless oil*
> *grated rind and juice 3 lemons*
> *2 tbsps runny honey*
> *60ml/2floz chicken stock.*

Toss the chicken in the seasoned flour and fry the pieces until well browned on all sides (about 10 minutes). Put in a single layer in a shallow baking dish, drizzle with the honey and sprinkle with the lemon rind. Pour the juice and stock into the dish and bake at 180C/Gas 4 for 35–40 minutes, till tender. Good hot and even better cold.

Tomato Confit and Basil Galettes

Actually, having decried the ridiculousness of individually plated items, I do think that these little tarts are quite a good idea. You have to assemble them on the spot, but if you take everything with you in little containers that won't be a problem.

> *6 large or 9 medium ripe plum tomatoes, peeled and thickly sliced*
> *olive oil*
> *6 rounds of puff pastry, about 15cm/6in across (or, if you use the ready rolled stuff, just cut it into squares. Do round off the corners as sharp corners break more easily and, after all, you will be transporting these in the boot of a car)*
> *12 sun-dried tomatoes in oil*
> *2 tsp tomato purée*
> *large handful fresh basil.*

Start with the tomatoes. You are trying to dry them off a bit so the flavour intensifies and they start to go a bit chewy, almost. Put them in a baking tin and drizzle with olive oil and some salt. Bake in a very low (160C/Gas 2) oven for about 1½–2 hours, checking every so often. You don't want them to cook and disintegrate. Allow to cool. Prick the pastry squares with a fork and bake at 170C/Gas 3 for about 8 minutes till golden. Turn them over halfway through so they don't rise too much and stay relatively flat. Whiz the sun-dried tomatoes with the tomato purée and some black pepper. When you come to the assembly line (but not before, because chopped basil goes black very quickly) chop the basil and stir a little into the tomato purée paste. Spread each pastry square with a little tomato paste, top with tomato slices and sprinkle with some more chopped basil.

Home Cured Beef Carpaccio

For the main course, I would go again for simple but luxurious. Serve this with masses of rocket and Parmesan and some lemon wedges, and if you want to, some hot baby new potatoes which you have either brought along and kept warm in a wide-necked vacuum flask, or cooked on the little camping stove behind the car. Yeah, right. Don't forget you will have to make this at least five days in advance. The quantities given actually make enough marinade for two, so why not do two and freeze the second fillet? This marinade recipe is based on one by Gary Rhodes, slightly adapted. If you like you can add more herbs to the marinade – rosemary or basil would be most successful, I think – or add brandy instead of the bitters, or use red wine, or add a couple of strips of orange peel – whatever. It's a jumping-off point, not a rulebook.

960g/2lb fillet of beef
125ml/4floz balsamic vinegar
125ml/4floz dark soy sauce
60ml/2floz Angostura bitters
4 tbsps Worcestershire sauce
4 cloves garlic, crushed
thyme
1 tbsp crushed black peppercorns
300ml/½ pint dry white wine
450ml/¾ pt olive oil
15g/½ oz sea salt.

Mix the marinade ingredients and sit the fillet(s) in it. Cover and refrigerate for at least four and up to eight days, turning frequently. Drain the meat and pat dry. Strain the marinade and check for seasoning (if you want to use it as a dressing, otherwise I would suggest a mixture of just dark soy, a little balsamic and some chopped fresh basil).

Orange and Almond Cake
This is a really versatile cake. It is smart enough to be served as a pudding, with lots of fresh berries (blueberries are especially good) and some crème fraîche, and yet robust enough (if you leave it in its tin) to be taken on picnics and served with hot black coffee or chilled champagne. Also, it's dead easy. And, as if you needed any more plus points, it's suitable for vegans. Not that that's necessarily a selling point (I don't know your friends).

2 large unpeeled oranges (and as you're cooking them whole, if you can get unwaxed, organic ones, so much the better)
6 eggs
250g/½ lb ground almonds
250g/½ lb sugar
1 tsp baking powder
pinch salt.

Boil the oranges for 2 hours. Oil and line a deep cake tin or square tin, and set the oven to 180C/Gas 4. Cool the oranges, cut open and pip, then purée in a blender. Beat the eggs and stir in all other ingredients, combining well. Pour into the tin and bake for an hour/hour and a half (this does depend on how wet your mixture was).

Chapter 10

Impromptu Entertaining

There is a real danger here that this turns into one of those irritatingly smug chapters which says, yes, now is the time to defrost the shepherd's pie you made a month ago when you had that leftover chunk of roast. This is dangerous nonsense. I certainly have never been that organised, and consider people who do that sort of thing worryingly anal. Anyway I haven't got a freezer large enough. I'm sure it's a different story if you live in the country and regularly stash away whole wildebeest, to come back to when you just can't face another fresh salmon. Darling. Impromptu entertaining is, to me, the sort of thing you can assemble from the cupboard at half an hour's notice, with perhaps a little assistance from the grocers at the tube station or the corner shop on your way home. 'Impromptu' implies that you have rashly asked your mates home for some food after the cinema, or that you decided at 5.30p.m., mildly hungover, that you can't actually face the pub after work and instead why don't they come back to yours. So not only do you have to make supper pretty well exclusively from what you have in the house or can find on the way home, but you also have to assemble it relatively speedily. On a slightly tangential note, impromptu entertaining almost always involves cooking what I serve if there are only going to be the two of us for a mid-week supper. Get home and then decide what to cook, rather than plan the menu weeks in advance – serendipity playing a large part in things. Did I pass the brilliant Italian deli on my way to the tube? Did the street market in Soho near work have a special on artichokes? Are those mushrooms in the fridge looking a little slimy, and those leftover lentils could do with being used up too? Et voilà – garlic mushrooms and lentils on toast. Impromptu entertaining is challenging because you have decided to offer your services as host at the shortest possible notice period.

So we're talking easy food. I'm afraid there is a certain amount of 'the handy tin that you should always have in your store cupboard', but again, there is nothing here that you won't be able to get from your local shop. One thing I would say is that, for impromptu food to feel like food and not just a snack (no matter how well put together a snack), you have to have at least one hot course. I would think that an assortment of charcuterie and bread, followed by cheese and maybe fruit, would be all very well and doubtless deeply nourishing, but I would still feel a bit – well, as if there was something missing. Which does have the advantage of sanctioning my face first dive into the freezer looking for ice cream.

There are various ways round the impromptu thing. The main one being, Throw Money At The Problem. Get some smoked salmon for first course, or a New Covent Garden soup – their carrot and coriander is reliably delicious, and you can pretty it up with a blob of crème fraîche and a sprinkle of chopped coriander. Or Parma ham and fresh figs (if you can find them). Or a bowl of peanuts (look, you asked these people home from the pub). You are not expected to give them eight courses.

For main course, one of my favourite things, although to be honest you can really only serve this to one or at the most two girlfriends, is to serve nothing but asparagus, in huge quantities, with either vinaigrette or hollandaise, and lots of ciabatta. I would only serve it to girls, I think, partly because most men would be less than thrilled at the prospect of a purely vegetarian supper, and secondly because the amount of asparagus you can eat if you truly love it is a really appalling amount – and no woman I know actively likes revealing her greedy side. I prefer my asparagus with vinaigrette, I think, as hollandaise rapidly becomes too rich to eat much of. Also, unless you buy it in a jar (and I sincerely advise you not to, because it always tastes curiously medicinal) it is quite time-consuming to make. Not difficult, but time-consuming. Vinaigrette, on the other hand, you can make up in huge quantities and it keeps forever. I did, however, once hear that you shouldn't keep whole garlic cloves in vinaigrette for longer than three days as after that they can harbour botulism. Every time I finish up my vinaigrette the garlic clove which falls into the salad at the end has turned blue, which I know can't be a good sign, but on the other hand I'm not dead yet. It's up to you. Fish it out, or don't fish it out.

Other tips for impromptu cooking, if you want something a bit more substantial, are things like fish, or breast of chicken in strips. Both cook in minutes. Fish is often better, I think, done simply rather than drowned in complicated sauces. Flash fry it in butter, adding a squeeze of lemon and some chopped fresh herbs and, if you like, a blob of crème fraîche, before serving with quickly boiled new potatoes. Or, from the starting point of a plain tomato sauce, add other flavourings – go Thai, with ginger and chillies; or Italian, with herbs and garlic; or Spanish, with orange rind and sherry. Chicken you can play with to your heart's content, depending on what you have in the cupboard and what you've been able to pick up on the way home. Especially since chicken breasts can be a bit boring. One of my favourites is Quick Moroccan chicken (flash fried with chillies, or chilli flakes, and, seeing as though we're in the storecupboard, honey, tomatoes, raisins and pinenuts). Chop fresh mint over if you have it. Or Quick Bourguignon (fried in butter with mushrooms, onion, garlic and bacon, then add red wine and a splash of port). Nigel Slater has many many good ideas for chicken, if you need further inspiration.

But for most of us, the great standby of impromptu cooking has got to be pasta. Hurray for pasta, where on earth would we be without it? It cooks in 10 minutes and goes with everything except possibly chocolate. I have to tell you, though, that there is a Maltese pudding of deep fried Ricotta ravioli, drained on kitchen paper and dredged with icing sugar and cocoa. Seriously, I think you have to be born there. If you are really stuck, you need nothing more than fresh sage, butter and Parmesan; or olive oil, garlic and chillies; or an egg, some ham and a bit of cream. And to be ruthlessly honest, I have all but given up making my own tomato sauce. If you want people to believe it's all homemade, then grate a courgette into the jar of pasta sauce and heat it till it's cooked, or top with some black olives or chopped fresh herbs. You could also stir it through rice, I suppose, but somehow that's less appealing.

And pudding? Oh for heaven's sake, buy ice cream. Do I even have to tell you? You can jazz it up any number of ways, with chocolate fudge sauce, or the Italian trick of pouring an espresso cup of seriously strong coffee over it (use your brain here, this will not go well with strawberry cheesecake ice cream, but it would be excellent over vanilla or hazelnut). Or in season, buy fruit. But don't buy mimsy little amounts of eight different kinds – find one fabulously good fruit, some gorgeously black red shiny cherries, or purple oozing blackberries, or really good sharp tangerines, depending on the season, and just pile them high on a plain white plate. The cherries would be good with some of those small thin squares of really good dark chocolate, at least 70% cocoa solids. The blackberries need a bowl of sugar and some proper double cream, or mascarpone. Be generous – don't just have two small bunches of grapes, have a whole bowl piled high. Profligacy and abundance in all things. Or – and this is my current favourite trick – go to the all-night garage and find several bags of the kind of sweets you had forgotten existed (unless you do a lot of motorway journeys). Wine gums (must be Marshalls), jelly babies, Revels, marshmallows, chocolate eclairs, Opal Fruits (now the disappointingly named 'Starbursts') and mint humbugs. Lots of places do pick 'n' mix, and though this can be ruinously expensive, the sheer joy of watching your smart friends eat a blue jelly spider the size of their hand will be worth it. Rip open many many bags and put the sweets pell-mell into a bowl. Serve with a flourish, calling it the bonbon dish. Frankly you will be amazed at how many strawberry bootlaces these people can eat.

What to Throw Together from the Cupboard

Big Tuscan Bean Soup
This only serves four really polite eaters, truly it's more like three. With thanks to Trixie Flory. Again you will see this is not really a recipe so much as a technique. I often add thinly sliced mushrooms to this, for more bulk, and serve it with a hunk of Parmesan for grating and some good olive oil for drizzling over at the end. You can chop some fresh basil or parsley in at the last minute too, if you're trying to impress. Word of warning – this soup is deceptively filling – it really is only suitable as a supper or main course, don't give it to people as a starter because (I think it's the pulses) it is fairly solid and expands deceptively in the tummy after you've eaten it.

Impromptu Entertaining

> *1 onion*
> *olive oil*
> *2 cloves garlic*
> *400g tin chopped tomatoes*
> *chicken stock (a cube is almost* de rigeur *here)*
> *tin cannellini or flageolet beans or chick peas, drained and rinsed*
> *spring greens, or Savoy cabbage, or frozen spinach, or grated courgette*
> *10–12 slices salami, or equivalent in Parma ham, or pancetta, or streaky bacon.*

Brown the onion lightly in the olive oil; if you are using pancetta or bacon, also cook them now, then add the garlic, tomatoes, stock, beans and quite a lot of black pepper (and mushrooms, if using). A good tip for the stock is not even to worry about dissolving the cube in water – fill the still-tomatoey tin with water, pour it into the pan and lob in the stock cube (squash it up a bit with your fingers). It will all boil down nicely, and after all we are looking for speed here not preciousness. Boil hard for 5 minutes till slightly thickened. Stir in the shredded greens and cook till softened. Add the cubed salami or ham, stir in till heated through and serve immediately with lots of ciabatta.

Spaghetti with Olive Oil, Garlic and Chilli

> *Enough pasta for 4 (read the packet, but about 350g/12oz)*
> *5 tbsps good olive oil*
> *4 small dried chillies (or less or more)*
> *2 cloves garlic, crushed*
> *1 bay leaf, crumbled*
> *½ tsp rosemary, chopped*
> *salt*
> *and if you like anchovies you can add one or two, chopped.*

While you are cooking the pasta, heat all the remaining ingredients in the oil over a low heat. Drain the pasta, reserving a little of the cooking water. Stir the pasta into the oil, adding a little of the reserved water if necessary to slacken it. Serve with Parmesan. If you happen to have an aubergine or a courgette lying about, cut into small cubes and fry separately till browned. Stir in with the oil. Even frozen peas can be usefully added.

Chocolate Fudge Sauce

>30g/1oz butter
>30g/1oz cocoa powder
>½ tsp vanilla essence
>2 tbsps water
>15g/½ oz sugar (optional, depending on how dark you want your sauce)
>1 tbsp golden syrup.

Combine and heat till melted and dissolved. The longer you boil it, the fudgier it becomes. Get out the vanilla ice cream and go.

The Relatively Smart

Grilled Radicchio or Mushrooms with Blue Cheese and Balsamic Vinegar

Again, more of a method than a recipe. This will serve four as a starter, and two as a main course. I had the mushroom version recently done on a barbecue, and it was sensational (plus the edges of the mushrooms kept all the amazing savoury juices inside).

>1 radicchio or 4 of those gigantic flat mushrooms
>creamy blue cheese (Gorgonzola or Dolcelatte are very good)
>balsamic vinegar
>ciabatta to serve.

Preheat the grill. Cut the radicchio vertically into four equal slices or if using the mushrooms, wipe clean of any dirt. (Tip: never peel mushrooms. Life is too short. You're going to cook them anyway, any lurking germs will be cremated then. I've never killed anyone with a dirty mushroom in my life yet.) Sprinkle each with about a teaspoon of balsamic vinegar. Top with a slice of blue cheese and grill on a baking sheet till golden and bubbling. This will not look very pretty (the radicchio goes grey and the cheese goes sort of pale green), but you will fight over the juices that are left on the tray. Serve with ciabatta for mopping.

Cheese Soufflé

This is based on the original Penguin Cordon Bleu recipe, but I have somewhat adulterated it. This really only serves 4 people if you're having it as a starter. I would say it serves 2–3 if you're having it as a main course, with salad and crusty brown bread (and HP sauce, if you're anything like my family). It goes very well, oddly enough, with really cold German white wine.

> 45g/1½ oz butter
> 30g/1oz flour
> 250ml/8floz milk
> 5 egg yolks
> 4 egg whites
> 4–5oz/125–150g strong cheese (eg Cheddar, Roquefort, Stilton, Gruyère, or whatever you have lying around the fridge looking old and scaly. You could even use goat's cheese, I suppose. Don't use too much Parmesan, though, I think it goes a bit acrid when there's too much.)
> salt, cayenne, paprika, nutmeg, black pepper, dry mustard powder.

Make a white sauce with the butter, flour and milk (see p. 37 for technique). Beat in the egg yolks off the heat. Work in the cheese, and season with salt (careful though, as the cheese will be salty), black pepper, cayenne, dried mustard powder, a bit of nutmeg – any or all of these that you fancy. Now for the clever part. If by any chance you are doing this ahead of time (you have been paying attention to the rest of the book, haven't you!) you can set it aside at this stage by cutting out a circle of plastic bag (yes, plastic bag, your Tesco carrier glut could finally see a dent) just slightly larger than the pan you've made the cheese sauce in, running it under the cold tap, and then pressing the wet side down onto the surface of the sauce. It feels truly horrible under your fingertips, I am warning you now. Leave overnight, if you want.

Butter the inside of a soufflé dish and set the oven to 180C/Gas 4. You cannot put a soufflé into a cold oven. (Also, make sure the rungs of the oven are set in such a way that there will be a bit of room for the soufflé to rise. How embarrassing to have to pull the beautiful top of your perfect creation off the roof of the oven because you set the rungs too high.) Beat the egg whites in a bowl till really stiff. There is no trick – no lemon juice, no copper bowl, no pinch of salt mumbo jumbo – just beat them. Although there is quite a good trick to check if they're stiff enough – you should be able to turn the bowl upside down and they stay stuck to it. For heaven's sake tilt the bowl gently and slowly at first to see if they're slipping around before you show off to your admiring audience by holding it over your head. With a metal spoon gouge out a spoonful of egg white and stir it into the cheese. This will slacken it a bit and make it easier to fold in the rest of the whites into the mixture. Using a figure of eight motion, and remembering every so often to scrape across the bottom of the bowl to get the shy and retiring cheese sauce up and over the egg whites, gently but firmly fold the egg whites into the cheese sauce. This is a lot easier than it sounds, I promise. It's much more complicated in the describing than it is in real life. You only need to see it done once to see what I mean. Get an aunt to show you.

Pour and scrape into the prepared soufflé dish and put in the hot oven. Leave for 15–20 minutes before checking. The top should be golden brown and maybe even dark brown in some places, and the underneath should be wobbly and a bit like runny scrambled egg. Serve at once to rapturous applause.

Once you've mastered the basic soufflé, you can start to mess about with it a bit. Stir some cooked spinach through the cheese sauce. Add some chopped ham, or a few chopped sun-dried tomatoes or olives. Put some cooked mushrooms in the base of the soufflé dish before topping with the cheese fluff. Or use less cheese at the beginning and stir in some flaked smoked mackerel.

Orange Chicken

(For John – the first thing I ever taught him to cook. Although this is so easy, calling it cooking is slightly stretching it.)

> 4–6 chicken joints, skin on
> 300ml/½ pint fresh orange juice (freshly squeezed is

Impromptu Entertaining

best, but carton will do)
grated rind of 1 orange
½ tsp paprika
tsp or more cayenne, Tabasco, harissa, chilli powder, chilli flakes or fresh red chilli
salt and pepper.

Stab chicken joints all over as deep as possible with a knife and place in one layer in a shallow, non-metal (because metal will react with the acidic orange juice) ovenproof dish. Mix the orange juice, orange rind, paprika, selected spice flavour, a little salt and some pepper. Pour over the chicken (it will come about halfway up the joints) and marinate overnight (or for as long as you have). Bake uncovered at 180C/Gas 4 for about an hour, basting at intervals. The chicken will develop a slightly burnt look. Sprinkle with parsley for bijou decorative effect. Good with baked potatoes and broccoli.

The best variation I ever did of this was to use blood oranges. The sauce was the most amazing dark ruby colour. John's variation on this is to thinly slice the orange from which he has taken the rind and put the slices into the marinade, and sometimes he adds red onion, cut into wedges. He also serves this with leek rice.

Leek Rice

Now. It always says on the side of the packet that 60g/2oz rice is enough for one individual portion. Hmmm. Not sure I believe them – what I tend to do for four people is measure out 240g/8oz like I'm told and then think, "that's never enough" and add a bit more for good measure. Anyway, you do as much rice as you think you need for four of you.

rice for four (see above)
2–3 leeks, trimmed
½ tsp curry powder
½ tsp turmeric or a pinch of saffron threads
knob of butter.

A word about washing leeks. They can be vilely gritty, and you will never, because of the leek's peculiar interlocking layered structure, ever get it all out. What I tend to do is cut them up first, after trimming off the gnarly whiskery bits, and then decide if I need to selectively wash or pull off rings which are particularly muddy. Also, when you cut them up – and this is a purely personal fad, so feel free to ignore it (oh and by the way it extends to all veg that you have to cut across, whether it be courgettes, carrots, celery, spring onions, parsnips, even bananas, whatever) – there is something about straightforward discs which tastes so dreary. It's far nicer to cut them on the diagonal, so you have longer flat surfaces. Anyway. Cut them however you like. It's your supper.

Cook the rice according to the packet instructions. While it's cooking, gently fry the leeks in the butter. When they're about 5 minutes from done (so after about 5–8 minutes gentle frying), add the curry powder and turmeric or saffron and cook until the leeks are soft and slippery. If you can get one or two of them to catch and caramelise a bit, so much the better. Drain the rice if it needs it, and stir it into the leek pan (much better this way than to put the leeks into the rice, this way you get every last drop of delicious curried butter). The turmeric or saffron will make the rice a glorious pale yellow which looks great with the green of the leeks. Check for seasoning.

Chocolate Fondue

This will knock their socks off, and it is so easy you scarcely even need a recipe.

> *200g/7oz bar dark chocolate (70% minimum cocoa solids please)*
> *250ml/8floz double cream*
> *splash vanilla essence or rum/brandy/Amaretto/Cointreau*
> *pinch cinnamon (optional)*
> *pinch salt.*

Snap the chocolate into a heatproof bowl. Heat the cream till boiling, pour over the chocolate and whisk madly (over a low heat if necessary, in a bain marie if you like, or in the microwave) until the chocolate has melted. Stir in the vanilla, cinnamon and salt and serve with any or all of the following:

- Fresh pineapple chunks

Impromptu Entertaining

- Strawberries
- Cherries
- Banana slices
- Orange wedges
- Amaretti biscuits
- Macaroons
- Marshmallows (a particular favourite).

Quick Spinach Risotto

Another of those recipes which is more of a method than a recipe. You can add more vegetables (stir in frozen peas, or broad beans), or add some cooked chicken, or crumbled bacon, or cheese (Fontina is nice, or Gruyère), or make it with one of the other Riso Gallo flavours. Infinitely flexible, infinitely delicious.

> *1 onion, sliced*
> *olive oil*
> *5 espresso cupfuls of flavoured risotto rice (see C List, p. 4), spinach flavour*
> *dash of nutmeg*
> *1–2 of those ready-washed pillow bags of baby spinach leaves*
> *sliced spring onion*
> *extra Parmesan, to serve.*

Fry the onion in the oil until softened, then add the rice. Stir around in the onion till warming up then add 10 espresso cupfuls of water (according to the packet you need double the volume of water as rice, but keep an eye on it, depending on the shape of your saucepan and the ferocity of the heat you may need more water). Add the nutmeg and let it bubble, stirring fairly often to make sure it's not catching on the bottom. You could add a splash of white wine too, if you liked, at this stage. When the rice is about 1 minute from ready (i.e. after about 9 minutes) dump the spinach into the pan (it will be very squeaky and bouncy so you will need to keep prodding it down and pushing it under the hot rice). Cook, stirring, until the spinach has wilted but is still nice and green. Check for seasoning, stir in the spring onion if using, and serve at once. Nice with a tomato salad for colour contrast.

Two Easy Tarts – Mushroom and Garlic; and Strawberry and Mascarpone

Basically here you are just making a giant vol-au-vent case which you subsequently fill with whatever takes your fancy.

350g/12oz packet ready rolled puff pastry.

Set oven to 180C/Gas 4. Unravel the pasty and score a rectangle on it fairly deeply about 2cm/1in in from the edge. Put on a baking tray and bake till golden. The inside will puff up like a giant pillow – prick it with a fork and push it down so the edges stay risen and form a lip, and you can spread the filling on the inside.

Mushroom and Garlic

> 500g/1lb mushrooms, wiped and thickly sliced
> 30g/1oz butter plus another little bit
> 2–3 cloves garlic, crushed
> grated rind 1 lemon
> 3 tbsps chopped fresh parsley
> 2 tbsps grated Parmesan.

Fry the mushrooms gently in the butter. After a bit they will give off masses of juice, and turn up the heat and boil that away hard so you are left with a fairly dry mixture. Now add the remaining butter, the garlic and lemon rind and toss about till you can really smell the garlic. Season with salt and pepper and stir in the fresh parsley. Pile into the pastry case, scatter with the Parmesan and put under the grill so the Parmesan just starts to catch. Serve at once.

Other Savoury Fillings

- A little ratatouille and some scrambled eggs (Elizabeth David's piperade)
- Sliced leeks and thinly sliced fennel, fried in butter till soft and then add a couple of tablespoons of cream and some crumbled Stilton
- Roasted red peppers and tomatoes, anchovies, black olives
- Red onion and thyme, slowly cooked in olive oil, with chunks of goats cheese and some walnut halves.

Strawberry and Mascarpone

> 250g/8oz mascarpone (one of those supermarket pots)
> grated rind and juice of an orange
> a little lemon juice
> 2–3 tbsps icing sugar
> 2–3 tbsps Cointreau
> strawberries
> chopped fresh basil (optional – it's a bit nouvelle cuisine but I like it).

Beat the mascarpone with the orange rind, orange juice, lemon juice and icing sugar. Flavour to taste with Cointreau and basil. It should be a nice spreading consistency, not too runny though. Pile into the pastry case and top with sliced strawberries. Scatter with the basil if desired.

Other Sweet Fillings

- Lightly stewed plums (in which case, flavour the mascarpone with sugar, lemon juice, marsala and maybe some vanilla)
- Mixture of red and whitecurrants (lovely, as they are so pretty – but they are quite sharp, so you might want to bump up the sugar in the mascarpone)
- Forgo the mascarpone altogether and just fill the pastry with apples cooked with cinnamon and cloves and a bit of sugar, and serve lots of cream on the side
- Sliced bananas, chocolate ice cream, chocolate sauce, flaked almonds, whipped cream.

You may be called upon to cater for a group of men watching the rugby or footy (who have thought to bring beer but nothing else). In this case you need something idiot proof to assemble, substantial (for blotting up all that beer), and which won't come to any harm if left in the oven for an extra half hour of injury time (or whatever it is that happens in sport). To be honest, there is a great deal to be said for dialling dinner in, or if you live too far out in the country, the oven bake pizza. Why kill yourself to provide nutritionally exemplary, gourmet meals when they are going to be scarfed down with one hand round the fork and the other round the beer tin? If you feel you must provide home cooking, most men like beef, so the quick beef stroganoff, if you've been able to get enough warning to buy some rump steak, will get votes, and it is a real treat.

Beef Stroganoff

Now the theory is that this serves four, but I'm not so sure. I think that's a bit optimistic, I would think more like three and possibly only two, if this is all that's on offer.

>   *500g/1lb rump steak, in 5cm/2in strips*
>   *Worcestershire sauce*
>   *30g/1oz butter*
>   *1 large onion, very thinly sliced*
>   *sliced mushrooms (however many you think – at least 8–10, and also, they bulk out the expensive beef very well, so will stretch this quite well).*

Put a good splash of Lea & Perrins over the meat. Melt the butter and cook the onion and mushroom till soft. Add beef and cook over a high heat till done. Meanwhile, make the sauce:

>   *2 tbsps butter*
>   *1 tbsp flour*
>   *125ml/4floz beef stock (get a cube out, for heaven's sake)*
>   *1 tbsp tomato purée*
>   *1 tsp Dijon mustard*
>   *pinch nutmeg*
>   *4–6 tbsps sour cream (or ordinary cream and a bit of lemon juice).*

Fry the flour in the butter, cook briefly then add the stock. Stir, then add the purée, mustard and nutmeg. Pour into the meat pan, heat through, stir in the cream, then serve immediately with rice.

Chicken and Sauce

Again, not so much a recipe as a method. Has the advantage of providing meat and vegetables in one fell swoop. Actually stirring a bag of baby spinach leaves into anything remotely stewy is quite a good way of getting green vegetables into the proceedings, and it makes the whole thing look a little less shop-bought. (They must be baby leaves because the big ones need washing and picking over – need I say more?)

> *4 chicken breasts, sliced*
> *oil*
> *1 onion, sliced, if you can be bothered with it, otherwise just leave it out*
> *1 clove garlic*
> *300g/11oz bag baby spinach leaves*
> *jar sauce – Chicken Tonight; or antipasto peppers in tomato sauce; or any of the proprietary brands of curry sauces (the Madhur Jaffrey range is especially good); or Tesco do a very good line of cook-in Thai sauces*
> *(I recommend the Green Curry one).*

Fry the onion (if using) in the oil, then add the chicken breasts and fry till just browning. Add the garlic, spinach and sauce. Heat through, bubble for 2–3 minutes till the spinach is nice and wilted and everything is piping hot, and serve with rice/noodles/potatoes as appropriate.

Baked Chocolate Bananas

> *4–6 bananas, not too ripe*
> *packet dark chocolate chips*
> *grated rind and juice one orange*
> *4 tbsps soft light brown sugar*
> *2 oz butter, in small pieces.*

Slice the bananas (diagonally is much nicer than straight rounds) and toss gently in a bowl with the chocolate chips and orange rind and juice. You could add a tablespoon or so of rum, too. Turn into a buttered china baking dish, scatter the butter and sugar over the top and bake at 200C/Gas 6 for about 15 minutes till the butter and sugar has melted and the edges of the bananas on top are just starting to catch. If you have some flaked almonds to hand and you like them, you could scatter them over the top at the same time as the butter and sugar. Serve with very cold cream.

Chapter 11

Cooking to Impress

One thing that will always get people oohing and aahing is if you have made your own pastry. I have never understood this as it is, in these days of the food processor, almost embarrassingly easy. Case in point? This delicious cheese, mustard and tomato tart. The pastry is rammed together in the blender in about a minute, and the whole thing is a complete knockout. It is a very good-tempered tart and sits quite happily in the switched-off oven for up to an hour after you have cooked it, staying warm until you're ready for it (it is much nicer warm than cold). Or the lard pastry in the treacle tart (which again, is another fantastically simple recipe), even though you don't use a blender for this.

Making your own bread is another sure-fire winner. I am not for one minute suggesting you make proper yeast-risen bread (I have tried all the recipes I have ever seen – brown, white, easy-blend yeast or fresh yeast, with a vitamin C tablet, with a tablespoon of treacle – and every loaf has had the consistency of a housebrick. And this in spite of a mother who used to make us bread on a weekly basis when we were small.) No – I'm talking about soda bread, which is so easy and so delicious. It's particularly good with smoked salmon, or with the smoked mackerel pâté from the *Tea* chapter.

If you've got an ice cream maker, making your own ice cream or sorbet gets rounds of applause too. This I have never understood, as all you have to do is assemble ingredients and leave the machine to do the rest. But somehow it's perceived as a big deal. Great, as far as I'm concerned. Plus, and I know you must be bored of this chant by now, it means you can Make It Ahead. (But funnily enough, not too far ahead; fresh ice cream seems to lose its perfume after about four days. It'll still be good, but just not as good as it could have been.)

Another good trick is to make just one special effort per course, and then surround the star ingredient with lavish supporting items. For example, this delicious onion marmalade gets star billing, and you add – buy – Parma ham, shavings of fresh Parmesan, cold cooked asparagus (either roasted or steamed), grilled artichoke hearts in olive oil (available from most Italian delicatessens already prepared, or in a jar from the supermarket and you will have to grill them yourself) and masses of fresh rocket. Arrange them on a large white china platter, and accompany with ciabatta. It is a completely brilliant first course and somehow the ingredients all together look so much more luxurious than if you had arranged them meanly on individual plates. Unfortunately I can't recall where I came across this recipe.

Tomato Tart

>*(6–8 as a starter, 3–4 as a lunch with salad)*
>*For the pastry:*
>*175g/6oz plain flour*
>*30g/1oz freshly grated Parmesan or Pecorino Romano*
>*½ tsp/ cayenne pepper*
>*90g/3oz butter, in cubes*
>*1 egg.*

Buzz the flour, cheese and pepper and then add the butter. Buzz again briefly then add the egg till it comes together in a mass. Press out thinly into a 12inch metal tart tin with a removable base (this is probably the most labour-intensive bit of this whole recipe). Prick with a fork and leave to rest in the fridge while you assemble the filling.
For the filling:

>*250g/8oz Gruyère, grated finely*
>*2–3 tbsps Dijon mustard*
>*12–16 good ripe tomatoes (depending on size, or you could use cherry tomatoes, in which case you'll obviously need more)*
>*olive oil*
>*pesto.*

Preheat the oven to 200C/Gas 6 and put your square baking sheet that is big enough to take the tart tin in to heat up at the same time. Spread the mustard evenly over the pastry base and sprinkle over the cheese. Slice the tomatoes across their equators about half a centimetre thick and discard the outermost slices (so all you have left are slices with a strip of skin round the edge). Arrange them in the case in overlapping circles (overlap them quite a lot as they shrink as they cook) but keep them only one slice deep. Brush gently with some olive oil and put in the oven on the baking sheet until the pastry is golden biscuity brown and the tomatoes are shrivelling and just catching at the edges. Slacken a couple of tablespoons of pesto with olive oil to make a runny consistency, then drizzle over the tart and return to the oven with the door closed till ready to eat.

Treacle Tart

For the pastry:

> 180g/6oz plain flour
> pinch salt
> 90g/3oz butter, cold from the fridge
> 30g/1oz lard, cold from the fridge
> cold water.

Sieve the flour and salt into a large bowl and then shave thin flakes of the fats into the flour with a sharp knife. Start to rub it into the flour with the tips of your fingers, lifting the mixture high and letting it fall back into the bowl to keep it airy. Stop as soon as it becomes heavy and starts to cling to your fingers – coarse large crumbs is the texture you are looking for. Add a couple of tablespoons of water and stir with a knife. Keep adding water, a little at a time, until the mixture just collects into a ball. Cover and chill for 20–25 minutes. Roll out and line a 12inch tart tin.

For the filling:

> 1 whole white loaf, stale, crusts cut off (or to be honest I usually use fresh, how often does one keep a stale loaf lying around?)
> 1 small tin golden syrup (only Tate & Lyle please, no supermarket imitations) – if you can warm the syrup up a little bit it will help it to spread more easily
> 1 egg, beaten with 1 tbsp water.

Set the oven to 220C/Gas 7. Paint the pastry with egg and bake it for about 12 minutes till golden brown. Remove from oven and lower the heat to 180C/Gas 4. Mix the crumbs and syrup, spoon/spread into case and bake for a further 15–20 minutes till the syrup is just on the verge of catching. Switch the oven off and leave to settle for 5 minutes before serving hot with custard, cream, or vanilla ice cream (or all three if you are feeling particularly greedy).

Asparagus, Parma Ham, Rocket and Parmesan with Onion Marmalade

> 3–4 medium onions, peeled and chopped (you can use red onions if you like)
> virgin olive oil
> 1 tsp brown sugar
> 1 tsp thyme leaves
> balsamic vinegar or crème de cassis
> salt and black pepper.

To accompany (per person):

> 2–3 slices of Parma ham
> 2–3 spears of asparagus
> 2 grilled artichoke hearts
> a handful of rocket leaves
> several shavings of Parmesan
> ciabatta.

Put enough oil in the bottom of a heavy-based saucepan to cover it to the depth of about a centimetre. Stir in the onions, and fry gently over a medium heat for about five minutes until the onions have gone glassy. Add the brown sugar, thyme and a couple of tablespoons of water. Cover, turn down the heat to low and cook slowly for anywhere between 30–60 minutes, stirring occasionally, till the onions are limp and brown, and there is not much liquid left. Stir in the vinegar or cassis and leave to cool. Check for seasoning.

To serve, put the onion marmalade in a pretty bowl in the centre of a china platter, and arrange the other ingredients round. Serve with plenty of ciabatta.

Peach Sorbet

This is only worth doing if you have really ripe, really succulent peaches.

> 100g/3oz caster sugar
> juice of 2 lemons
> 4 large or 6 smaller very ripe peaches (if you can get white ones, better yet)
> 1 tbsp Amaretto or brandy (optional).

Skin the peaches and buzz in the food processor with the other ingredients. Turn into the machine as per instructions, or freeze in a Tupperware container, beating from time to time to avoid ice crystals.

The success of entertaining is normally measured by how much *you* and your guests enjoy yourself. If you are entertaining to impress you need to adjust *your* perception of the event. For a start, you should decide upon which of your skills or attributes you wish to highlight. If you want to be seen as a conversationalist par excellence, then you should work out topics of interest, and practise your listening skills. If you want to show off your soufflé, practise your whisking and serving.

Be in control and, more importantly, be comfortable with your surroundings. Do not be seen to be trying too hard.

Cooking a good meal and behaving with good manners should impress your guests, whoever they are. However, in order to be truly impressive you need to have some solid behavioural foundations. This is in addition to a good recipe and a few topics of conversational gambit. Moving beyond this may require the use of a self-improvement book of which there are thousands.

Impressing a Boss

If your aim is a general impression of all round 'good eggness', then choose somewhere you feel comfortable with. You should ask questions and listen to the answers. Do not just think of your next witty or insightful remark, while the boss gives you an answer.

If you are looking to further your career in some respect, then talk knowledgeably about the issues facing your business in the wider world. Do not backstab colleagues or perceived opponents. Do not resort to having several job offers or that MBA application form lying around unless you mean to use it.

Cooking to Impress

When choosing a menu ensure that they will like it and that you can cook it. The balance between a consideration of their favourite food and a show of your personal characteristics is important. Avoid toadying.

Impressing a Potential Partner

A boy who can cook, has a pet, calls his mum on the phone regularly and is a member of Greenpeace, should be impressive enough. Add a good sense of humour, the ability to tango and a knowledge of fine wine and you'll probably find people who will fight for him. This person's female equivalent will demonstrate similar social characteristics of skill and grace and will probably have the resolve of a modern day Emily Pankhurst.

Assuming that you are a mere mortal, then more guidance is necessary for the first date. Do not get drunk, do not become aggressive or make clumsy sexual suggestions.

Food is a normal way to begin and sustain a relationship. Dinner is more formal and pressurised than lunch. A weekday lunch tends to have a time limit attached to it and sex is out of the question. Breakfast is downright unusual, though possibly a weekend brunch before another activity might do. Inviting someone round for tea is a good idea. It shows that you appreciate the finer and simpler things in life from an older and gentler time. It also saves a lot of cooking if this worries you, as some good biscuits and a sandwich will often suffice. Whatever you cook, you should be able to cook it quickly. You do not want to leave a new date rummaging around your living room while you are wilting in the kitchen. Avoid soup and spaghetti and do not slurp.

Occasions where there will just be the two of you can be a little stilted. Imagine if the evening is not going well, and you have only opened your mouth to change feet. You have only just served the first of four courses and there are still two hours before anyone can politely leave. What do you do? If you feel that leaving the two of you together at an early stage in your relationship is a bad idea, there are ways around this.

Inviting other people can provide some cover. However, consider who to invite. If they are obnoxious it will reflect badly on you. You also need to make sure that extra people do not feel like excess baggage. Another idea is to have some sort of engagement arranged. A trip to the theatre or an exhibition. Going to the cinema is a good idea in theory. There is a natural gap for silence, and something to talk about later.

If you decide to go to a restaurant, ensure it is not too formal. Make sure both of you are able to eat the food, a Mongolian steak house is not where the sensitive vegetarian wants to eat. Choose a restaurant which is not too noisy, if you want to actually speak to each other, and make sure you can afford to pay your way.

The bill payment is a can of worms for some. Who pays on these occasions, the male, female, or both? The answer depends on who has invited who, and one's attitudes to splitting the bill. Further complication can be added if one party is significantly more wealthy than the other. Rules for this kind of thing are difficult to apply. If you demand to pay, then you may leave your date feeling uneasy. If you are choosing the restaurant and the wine then make sure you tell your date that it is your treat and therefore you will pay. If you just want to go out and choose somewhere together then it is more probable that the bill should be split. Payment or non-payment should not be taken as a rebuttal or acceptance of sexual advances.

Conclusion

In essence, entertaining is about welcoming people into your world. What we hope to have achieved with this book is to help make that world as formal or informal as it needs to be. Whether we like it or not, society conforms to certain 'rules' and they are there to ensure safe passage through certain cultural minefields. If we stick to the rules then there is a diminished chance of us offending anybody.

We hope that this book will enable you to host a number of different parties, dinners, lunches, suppers, and weekend parties with enjoyment, ease and satisfaction. We have discussed the niceties of social rules to help you avoid grave social faux pas, provided fashionable formats to help you be in vogue and have supplied more pragmatic tips which should make your parties a runaway success. Most social occasions have a measure of all three of the above. Our aim was to give you some of the rules, a dash of the fashionable, and a lot of the practical.

The success of good entertaining, regardless of your motivation, is dependent on avoiding selfishness. Thinking of others before you think of yourself. Above all, it is about efficiency, maximum impact with minimum effort.

Financial considerations should not scupper party considerations. Even students with a penchant for more than corned beef hash and tequila can productively entertain. They manage it by keeping the food simple and balance the economics by insisting that everybody brings a bottle.

If the guests and the conversation establish the right ambience, then you can worry a little less about the consistency of your beurre blanc.

List of Recipes

	Page
Apple, Date, Ginger and Garlic Chutney	105
Asparagus, Parma Ham, Rocket and Parmesan with Onion Marmalade	139
Baked Amaretti Peaches	22
Baked Chocolate Bananas	135
Baked Courgettes with Tomato and Parmesan	97
Banana Bread	45
Beef Stroganoff	134
Big Tuscan Bean Soup	124
Bloody Marys	11
Cheese Sablés	93
Cheese Soufflé	127
Chicken and Sauce	134
Chicken Roasted with Tomatoes, Potatoes and Olives	28
Chilli, Lime and Coriander Butter for Corn	111
Chinese Pork	104
Chocolate Fondue	130
Chocolate Fudge Sauce	126
Chocolate Pavlova	33
Chocolate Sorbet	78
Chocolate Swiss Roll with Nutella	40
Cinnamon and Walnut Streusel Cake	14
Coffee Ice Cream	79
Coriander Salsa	111
Courgette Confetti	32
Courgette 'Snails'	73
Creamy Chicken, Leek and Mushroom Pie	24
Crostini with Roasted Green Peppers, Cumin and Black Olives	91
Cumin Roasted Carrots	32

List of Recipes

	Page
Dukkah	51
Easy Apple Cake	47
Fish Pie with Peas	36
Fishcakes	13
Flapjacks	116
Fresh Broad Beans, Peas and Parma Ham	76
Fruit Cobbler	39
Garlic Mushrooms	98
Giant Oven Chips	22
Glazed Garlic Mushroom and Asparagus Crêpes	64
Gratin Dauphinois	101
Green Beans with Ham and Tomato	97
Grilled Radicchio or Mushrooms with Blue Cheese and Balsamic Vinegar	126
Hollandaise Sauce	66
Home Cured Beef Carpaccio	118
Hot Honey Mustard Barbecue Sauce	110
Indian Potatoes	104
Jane's Chocolate Brownies To Die For	48
Kedgeree	12
Lamb Tagine with Prunes	98
Leek Rice	129
Lemon Honey Chicken	117
Lemon Surprise Pudding with Blackcurrants	54
Ma Kirkpatrick's Barbecue Sauce	110
Macaroni Cheese with Bacon	39
Mary's Knees	91
Mince Round	38
Mushroom and Garlic Tart	132
My Mum's Whisky Cake	46
Orange and Almond Cake	119
Orange Chicken	128
Orange Cornmeal Muffins	15
Orange Frangipane Pudding with Poached Orange Slices	70
Palmiers	51
Pasta with Wild Mushroom and Tomato Sauce	73
Peach Sorbet	139
Peach, Orange and Basil Barbecue Sauce	110
Peanut Butter Cookies	41
Pecan Pie Squares	74
Pesto Quiche	117

Debrett's New Guide to Easy Entertaining

	Page
Pineapple Custard Tart	28
Plain Grilled Chicken	31
Pommes au Beurre	25
Pork Marengo	21
Quick Spinach Risotto	131
Quick Spinach Soup	27
Raspberry Jam	16
Roast Monkfish with Bacon and a Red Pepper Sauce	68
Roasted Green Beans	69
Roasted Vegetable Couscous	77
Roasted Yellow Pepper Soup with Feta, Mint and Tomato	21
Salmon Koulibiac	95
Salsa Verde	31
Scones	15
Seared Moroccan Salmon	76
Smoked Mackerel Pâté	45
Smoked Salmon Scrambled Eggs	12
Spaghetti with Olive Oil, Garlic and Chilli	125
Sticky Upside Down Cake	106
Strawberry and Mascarpone Tart	132
Thai Fish Curry	53
Three Colours Red Chicken Skewers	96
Tomato Confit and Basil Galettes	118
Tomato Tart	137
Tomato, Butterbean and Pesto Soup	115
Treacle Tart	138
Turkey, Tomato and Ricotta Lasagne	100
Watercress Roulade with Horseradish and Smoked Trout	23
Yorkshire Pudding	26